CRIME OR EMERGENCY

53rd State Press
Brooklyn, New York

53SP 07
Published December 5, 2009

ISBN 978-0-9817533-6-2
Library of Congress Control Number: 2009941104

53rd State Press
Brooklyn, New York
www.53rdstatepress.com

CRIME OR EMERGENCY

and

THE LOST ACTS OF CRIME OR EMERGENCY

Sibyl Kempson

53rd State Press
Brooklyn, New York

Crime or Emergency was originally developed as an adaptation of the novel Reena Spaulings by the Bernadette Corporation (MIT Press/Semiotext(e), 2005). It was presented as a workshop production at Dixon Place in 2005, with the following cast:

Stage Directions	Camille Habacker
Lacey	Johanna S. Meyer
Donnamarie	Kourtney Rutherford
Howard	Jason Schuler
Sonja	Emily Sundblad
Sean Crosby/Announcer	Matthew Swan
Cowboy	Eben Moore
Milcha	Sibyl Kempson
Figgie	Mike Iveson, Jr.
Mary Oliver	Susie Sokol
Small Cowboy Statue	Andrew Dinwiddie
Large Cowboy Statue	Jim Fletcher

In 2007, *Crime or Emergency* received the Mondo Cane! Commission from Dixon Place, and was produced there with the following cast:

Lacey	Kate Benson
Donnamarie	Eleanor Hutchins
Sean Crosby/ Small Cowboy Statue	Alex Delinois
Howard	Jason Schuler
Sonja	Kourtney Rutherford
Announcer	Matthew Swan
Cowboy	Brian Mendes
Milcha	Sibyl Kempson
Figgie	Mike Iveson, Jr.
Garry	Richard Maxwell
Mary Oliver	Susie Sokol
Large Cowboy Statue	Jim Fletcher

Lighting Design	Casey McLain
Dramaturgy/Directorial Assistance	Suzanne Davies
Sound Design	Carmen Borgia

Crime or Emergency was further developed at the Fusebox Festival in Austin, TX in April, 2009, and in the Soho Rep Studio Series in January, 2008, with a reduced cast of Mike Iveson, Jr. and Sibyl Kempson. Directorial guidance from John Collins and Andrea Stover. It premiered at P.S. 122 in December, 2009, concurrently with the publication of this volume.

Before Crime or Emergency (Bernadette Corporation)

Before Crime or Emergency,
Sibyl was borrowing cars,
building costumes at night
for burgeoning theater companies,
birthing plays of considerable
boldness with giant characters,
being a confident performer,
banging drums in a country
band, chopping wood and
working for Bernadette Corporation.
Brought in to carry the dialogue
for a bunch of chapters in Reena
Spaulings, she brought charm
to the book and class, too.
The bit with the zombie cowboy
grabbing a bite at the cemetery,
the basketball champ at the hospital,
the boating disaster with the couple,
are some of the better cases
of her borrowing from her own constructions.
The scenes that became the core
and broke the chains of frustration
were brand new concepts:
the boxed ear conversation
and the Bruce Springsteen concert.
The biology and chemistry of theater
will never bridge the chasm
between the chairs of an audience
where each brain is contained

in its own bunker of concentration.
The brightest approach is to cause
more breakage and cleave
the greatest bones of the carcass
before the eyes of the captivated
bench. Great cuts
of beef cram the stage.
These are burned and carved,
broiled and cauterized til the show
becomes, when the smoke clears,
a kind of barbaric cuisine,
a banquet for conquerors who are perhaps
broken by their conscience or simply
broken, wild. A craving
blossoms in the corpse of each.
And the belly of each is a cave,
an empty bucket when they come.
Sibyl, born in a cyclone
like Dorothy into beauty and color,
looks backwards from her crimson
podium at her beige cohorts
and begins to cry. "I didn't
know it would be so cruel,
this business of coup de theatre,
but I love it and can't stop.
I believe in the macho competitive.
Whether you bail or continue,
my balls are more convincing
than some boy-bitches' concept
of bang-up, cutting-edge drama.
I want balloons and confetti
in every blast of conversation
if not a broadside cannonade.

It's bigger than this room, closer
to the bone than calcium tablets,
more of a boast than a claim.
A show that brags and carps,
that's the bag I'm carrying."
At this the birds were calmed.
The black and roiling clouds
betook themselves from the city's
banks and furthest coastlines.
A beaver paused its chewing
and breathed a sigh of calm.
In the branches, nothing cracked,
no boot or creature stirred.
A bus came to a stop.
Bubblegum was given to a child.
A blindman's cane was suffered
to brush the cashmere pantleg
of a billionairess. Chanel slacks.
If theater is a barrel of chimps,
based as it is in comedy
and the bathetic crowd-pleasers
that the Bowery churned out
by hook or by crook, Sibyl's
boils a quite caustic
bouillon in its dramatic cup.
The bark is at least as complex
as the bite, strong candy
for us banana-loving creatures.
No beginner in the conflicts
of love, she blends the comforts
of bed with the cheesy aroma
that foretells a brain in crisis.
Brecht would clap and hoot

at these botched ceremonies,
which bring to mind Céline
at his best, a monster with cancer.
Her body is the center of these shows,
the battlefield, not the conceptual
body but hers. Collapsing or
bounding from the corners, it struts,
bends or creaks, depending
on the barometer and compass it's using.
Butt-first she may enter, crude
but classy, a drag queen whose
background is completely female,
a king in borrowed clothes,
Zeus between carnal
forays, a barker at a carnival,
a Brenda, a Cleopatra, a Medusa.
Belt cinched tight,
she busts into a rollicking chanson
with blinkers and clangers on.
No brooding possible in a climate
of bulls and cows on the go,
bellowing, push, counter-push,
blow up, give up, continue,
breakfast. In fact it's charged,
this backyard cacophony, with ions
of a boisterous clarity. Robards
is a blowhard in a coma. An American
brand of civic manhood.
Pacino is a braised carrot
bundled in careful recipes,
often bearded and callow.
McQueen is bad and clean,
and a little backwoods. Clint

Eastwood is beyond childhood.
Brad Pitt is a chime
dangled in a breezy canyon.
The bong-hit Clooney
bubbles until it coughs smoke.
Penn's beaming and cleft
features are the boulders of his craft.
Kempson's bravado is contagious:
you breathe, it comes in . . .

CRIME OR EMERGENCY

This play is for Phyllis Dickens

A Play taking place in Contemporary Times

Characters

LACEY, a Nurse Practitioner
DONNAMARIE, a Medical Patient
SEAN CROSBY, Power Forward for the Dallas Mavericks
HOWARD, Hospital Administrator
SONJA, Public Relations Assistant at Schoenwandt Architecture Firm, LLC., girlfriend to Howard
ANNOUNCER
COWBOY, Intimate associate of Donnamarie
MILCHA, Cabaret Songstress, sister to Sonja
FIGGIE, Assistant to Milcha
GARRY, an additional Assistant to Milcha
Other Assistants to Milcha
MARY OLIVER, Journalist, Poet
SMALL COWBOY STATUE
LARGE COWBOY STATUE
DR. NANCY HASTINGS, retired Throat Surgeon, Negotiations Consultant, amateur sculptress
CHARLES HASTINGS, her long-suffering husband
PAUL PIANO TUNER
STATE TROOPER
Convalescents
Friday night Crowds
Many Dogs or Goats
Audience Members at a Supper Club
Lawyer
NURSES UNION
REVIEW PANEL

Note on the text

"//" indicates the interruption of the succeeding line onto the current line, so people are speaking over one another Caryl Churchill style.

SCENE 1.

A hospital room. Dallas, TX. DONNAMARIE and LACEY. An examination is taking place.

LACEY: Okay, just lay on back and I'll start the measurements. That's good. When was the last time you had this checked?

DONNAMARIE: About two years ago.

LACEY: You should really have this checked more often than that.

DONNAMARIE: Like how often?

LACEY: Every six months.

DONNAMARIE: Two years isn't that much longer than six months.

LACEY: Oh, no?

DONNAMARIE: No.

LACEY: Okay.

DONNAMARIE: Not when you've got an HMO breathing down your neck.

LACEY: Yeah, I hear that all the time.

DONNAMARIE: So how is it?

LACEY: This job?

DONNAMARIE: No.

LACEY: Oh. Well, we'll have to wait for the lab results.

DONNAMARIE: Come on. Don't give me that crap. You see this all the time, you're so fermiliar with all the different situations.

LACEY: Whatever.

DONNAMARIE: Yeah. You can tell me exactly what's going on just by looking at it. I know how you people are. You can but you won't. You don't want to have to deliver the bad news. So you just do your poking around and jabbing this into that and then you take your gloves off and go on your lunch break – I can even smell it, it's sloppy joes or manwich.

LACEY: I think we ordered baked ziti and Italian food, actually.

DONNAMARIE: Yeah, smells great. Smells real fucking great in a fucking HOSPITAL with all the body parts. Enjoy.

LACEY: Thanks, I will.

DONNAMARIE: Enjoy your fucking lunch!

LACEY: Try to have a good afternoon.

DONNAMARIE: Fucking jew!

LACEY: I'm not Jewish. Put that down.

DONNAMARIE: Oh, you're not? What about this!

LACEY: I already said put it down. I can call security.

DONNAMARIE: Go ahead, bitch. You Jew bitch.

LACEY: Okay STOP!

DONNAMARIE: No way, bitch!

LACEY: Hey –

DONNAMARIE: No way in HELL!

LACEY: *(goes to the intercom and buzzes calmly but furiously)* I'll need some help in here –

DONNAMARIE: No way in HELL bitch.

LACEY: *(into the intercom)* Hi, can somebody?

DONNAMARIE: You and me, we're goin to the end of the line!

LACEY: I think it's a code green 305 I've got in here – *(deciding to make a run for it into the hallway)* Oh, God –

DONNAMARIE: We'll see it through!

They run through the corridors of the hospital, Lacey running, Donnamarie chasing.

LACEY: Jesus. Oh, my God. Can't anyone see her scalpel!

It's all happening too fast for anyone to help. Trays of meds are overturned, weakened people hobbling along the various wards with IV drips are pushed aside or knocked over.

LACEY: *(cont'd)* Oh God! This is happening too fast! Uh! That whole tray of meds! Watch out! Move that IV drip! Oh . . . sorry! Oh! I need some help . . . I need some help . . . Uh, she's gaining on me! HELP!

SCENE 1A.

As they run, the cool linoleum tile floor of the hospital slides back, revealing a rougher concrete with yellow parking parameters. The back wall of the stage tips forward as, with hydraulic swiftness and silence, massive square concrete columns of disconcerting thickness rise up out of the stage floor to meet it. The back side of the wall is also concrete with parking spaces and it splits the space into two levels: an upper and lower deck, 4 and 5 respectively. Hundreds of glossy cars and SUV's – many with moonroofs – arrive from the wings, filling the parking spaces above and below. They are mostly BMW, Mercedes Benz, and Lexus brands. The stage lights on the upper level blaze to an extraordinarily intense degree, and projections of merciless blue sky with the tops of a few trees peeking over the barriers of the edge further indication of the top deck of the parking garage. Panels in the walls along the sides of the house and in the boxes on the mezzanine slide silently upward into the ceiling and the noses of hundreds more cars – mostly Nissan, Toyota and Acura Legends – pull into the theater, driverless, and stop. The walls in the house of the theater have been cemented over and thick cylindrical but square columns installed, and now make sense – the feeling of a parking garage is evident. It is a steamy day and heat radiates off the hoods of the baking cars on the upper level. Those sitting in the mezzanine will experience an unusually uncomfortable rise in temperature, while audience members with orchestra seats will remain cool and comfortable.

LACEY: *(cont'd)* Oh! Where does this go? Oh! The parking garage!

Lacey races lumberingly up the open stairwell from level 4 to level 5 into the midday oven, her white lab coat flying open, her id tag flapping up into her face.

LACEY: *(cont'd)* Level 4 . . . Level 5 . . . losing my breath . . . Limbs are heavy . . . the upper deck. Okay. Ugh! It's like an oven up here! Uh!

She makes a panicked survey of the parking deck and, not seeing a sufficient hiding place, decides to push on.

LACEY: *(cont'd)* Lexus, Mercedes, Toyota . . . THERE'S NOWHERE TO HIDE!

Behind her, a glass and stainless steel elevator shoots menacingly to the upper deck from underneath the stage. Heavy polished elevator doors marked by a large '5' skate open and Donnamarie reenters resuming hot pursuit through the black and silver cars.

DONNAMARIE: BAAH!

LACEY: Jesus. Oh, my God. Can't anyone see her scalpel! Hey, wait a minute! Aren't you Sean Crosby of the Dallas Mavericks – can't YOU help me!

Lacey has stumbled across SEAN CROSBY of the Dallas Mavericks. He is lying on his side in one of the designated handicapped parking spots. His arm and shoulder are blistered and burned from laying on the asphalt of Level 5, which has reached its peak temperature of 120° Fahrenheit. Those seated in the mezzanine should be able to relate to his distress. Nearly breathless, Lacey stops to talk to him.

DONNAMARIE: Oh, I know this guy. Remember me from that race that time? That was fun. A lot of fun.

LACEY: Can you help me?

SEAN: I'M RRREALLY FREAKED OUT.

DONNAMARIE: Don't help her! I'm GETTING her!

SEAN: DO YOU KNOW WHAT TIME IT IS? I CAN'T FIGURE IT OUT. I THOUGHT IT WAS LATER? HUH?

DONNAMARIE: Let's do it again sometime. Okay?

SEAN: WHAT?

DONNAMARIE: Go to a race. Only let's go together instead of just meeting up there. Okay?

SEAN: I FEEL LIKE I'M NOT GOING TO BE ABLE TO TALK TO MY KIDS WHEN I GET HOME. AND IT'S SO BAD CAUSE I DON'T EVEN KNOW, AT THIS POINT, IF I EVEN HAVE KIDS LIKE I THOUGHT I DID.

DONNAMARIE: You could pick me up at my house or I could come pick you up. Let me know.

LACEY: Just leave him alone. He's a mess. These are second or third degree burns – look at these blisters – the surface of this parking deck must be at its peak temperature – about 120° Fahrenheit. There's no telling how long he's been here. And clearly there's some problem with medication. I can help him, but you have to let go of the knife, and let go of the idea that you're going to get me back by hurting me physically.

DONNAMARIE: *(gleefully reminded)* Shut up, bitch! Shut up and RUN!

LACEY: Oh, my back hurts. Oh fuck!

DONNAMARIE: That's right! You better run, fatass!

LACEY: Where the fuck is my boss?

DONNAMARIE: Hah ha!

LACEY: Where is Howard?

Her cry echoes through the theater. Lights out.

During the lengthy blackout that follows, the temperature of the theater returns to normal. We hear sounds of water slapping lazily against the side of a boat and of other, outdoors sounds. Then we start to hear the sound of a woman softly humming. It's a meandering, unfamiliar tune and it sounds very intimate, as if the woman was sitting very close.

SCENE 2.

When the lights come up we find that the stage has been flooded with water – moving water. It's a river. (What about the bank? Is it visible?) A boat named the Gypsy Countess glides along on the river in the late, late afternoon of the same day. It is her maiden voyage. HOWARD steers the boat. Next to him sits his girlfriend, SONJA: an exotic foreign woman, possibly Israeli, possibly Argentinean, possibly Czechoslovakian, who is some years younger than Howard. She stares intently off into the distance.

HOWARD: Listen I'm getting hungry, I've been at the wheel all day long and I'm the only man on this boat, and now you've got to look to feeding me somehow. There's plenty of food in the hold, can't you look in there and see if you might make me up a little something?

SONJA: A little something to eat, you mean?

HOWARD: Well, yes. Yes, and little something. You know. You know me, I don't eat much, but I'll tell you what this boat going sure takes it out of you. I need to learn. I should have taken a class.

SONJA: I was working with that woman uptown, and she belongs to a yacht club in the Hamptons, you know they've got kids and the boy takes classes there during summers and they needed the kid's medical forms and such, so I had to fax it in, but there was a whole packet there about boating safety and different kind of knots, like tying knots not the speed, a sheepshank, and maritime terms and everything, and it didn't even occur to me to make a copy for ourselves or anything like that.

HOWARD: Geez. You really should've.

SONJA: Pff! I know, that's what I'm saying. Christ, I didn't think of it. You look so cute over there, can you please give me a kiss?

HOWARD: I can't right now, the current's strong here, I really have to hold the wheel tight.

SONJA: You're so strong.

HOWARD: Thanks, it's nice when you tell me that kind of thing.

SONJA: So you want supper . . .

HOWARD: Yes . . .

SONJA: Well, I mean I just don't really feel like it. I mean, I like just lying here. I really need this. It's been a lot of stress. Does it have to be something that's cooked? Do you like the Vienna Fingers?

HOWARD: The cookies?

SONJA: No, the sausages. Don't you need protein?

HOWARD: Pff. I can do it . . . So who was that guy you were talking to the other night?

SONJA: Oh, I knew you saw that! Well, you know he started tickling me when we stepped outside . . .

HOWARD: What do you mean

SONJA: He ran up behind me as soon as I got out of the door and started tickling me that's what.

HOWARD: Where?

SONJA: Right by the car –

HOWARD: No I mean where on your body

SONJA: Oh, you know, around the waist or whatever. It was crazy. I felt like I was in high school all over again. It was right in front of Stevie too. I was embarrassed!

HOWARD: What did you do?

SONJA: I squealed. What are you supposed to do when someone's tickling you who's never touched you before?

HOWARD: I don't know. I don't know what the standard norms are.

SONJA: Yeah mean either.

HOWARD: Fff.

SONJA: He kept on doing it in the car too. I was sitting in front?

HOWARD: Does he know you're with me?

SONJA: I don't think so. That'd be weird if he did.

HOWARD: . . . Doesn't that give you the creeps?

SONJA: Yeah, but I think he's harmless. I think he just likes me and he doesn't know how to touch women. Or talk to women, once he realizes he's talking to one or whatever. But you know me. I don't like strangers to look at me let alone touching me.

HOWARD: Well he's not exactly a stranger –

SONJA: He sort of is.

HOWARD: What did it feel like? To you? I mean, I'm making an assumption here about the frequency of you being touched by men other than me. But I'm really just curious, passing the time.

SONJA: It was shocking, certainly, but I think it was his way of testing the waters. It was unfortunate, but do you mean beyond all that what did it feel like?

HOWARD: Yeah –

SONJA: His fingers were intrusive but not . . . unwarm?

HOWARD: Okay, I know what you're saying. Sure.

SONJA: It was just his fingers. Had there been palms involved it would have been a different story.

HOWARD: Oh yeah. How so?

SONJA: I don't know, exactly, but it would have been a different proposal altogether. You mean would my response have been different?

HOWARD: Well . . .

SONJA: I can't tell you that for sure. I mean as it was I stiffened right up. Even if we had been alone I would have. But if we had been alone and he put his whole hands on me? Or tried to kiss me? Honestly, darling I don't know. I probably would have really freaked out. Jesus, I don't know.

HOWARD: I don't like this.

SONJA: In a way it's like living in one house for a while, and it's a small house, and then having a dream that the house has a whole different section that you never knew about or saw before, like a crazy huge screened-in porch, but really elaborate. With different rooms and furniture you didn't think existed, even with new views onto completely different property than what you had heretofore known to have surrounded the house. Everything is very dark green with rainy foliage rich and crowding in beyond the screens of the porch. And it's homey, like it's not new, it's just been a secret that's been kept from you for whatever reason, and you see that life has been going on here all along without you, without needing you, green astro turf underfoot, full ashtrays, papers and pens, and there's a large rabbit with human looking eyes and big teeth that knows how to manipulate by smiling, and you try to masturbate there because it's so dewey and sexual but you get interrupted . . .

HOWARD: Jesus.

SONJA: I'm sorry.

HOWARD: I mean you're telling me this and I'm also looking at the sky up ahead here – do you see? And it's too much.

SONJA: Well, I don't think anything's going to happen with me and him, if that's what you're worried about.

HOWARD: What about the sky?

SONJA: I know. I was seeing it.

HOWARD: Do you think that's a warning?

SONJA: No, that's only in the morning.

HOWARD: I think it's a warning about this relationship, that it's headed toward rocky waters.

SONJA: It's okay to go through rocky waters together.

HOWARD: Do you think we could live on this boat?

SONJA: Oh, shit, I don't know – I hadn't thought about it.

HOWARD: When you live on a boat everything has to go in its little place. You can't just leave things lying around.

SONJA: I won't leave anything lying around – what are you saying?

HOWARD: Oh, God, I'm just trying to talk nonsense to get you to get me some food. I don't know what else to do.

SONJA: Look, why don't you just let me take the wheel and you can go get the food for yourself? I just mean that I can never seem to please you exactly when it comes to food, and I always get my feelings hurt that way. I'm talking again and again. So please just get it yourself and I'll hold the wheel?

HOWARD: What? I like the food you cook, I just make suggestions –

SONJA: I don't like 'suggestions.' I want you to rave about it, what I'm cooking for you. Because I can't cook or prepare food for someone I love without it being an expression of how I feel about them, just the same as I can't have sex with someone I love in a casual way.

HOWARD: Uch. It's so heavy that way. You're very demanding.

SONJA: So are you, at least when it comes to food. I'm not your mother.

HOWARD: Oh, please . . . c'mon, I'm so hungry!

SONJA: *(rising for the first time from her reclining position)* Here, let me take the wheel.

HOWARD: No, you can't do it, it pulls to the side –

SONJA: *(grabbing at the wheel)* Let me do it

HOWARD: *(pushing her away)* No

SONJA: *(wrenching the collar of his shirt passionately)* What are you talking about

HOWARD: Let go!

He pushes her again, this time more violently. She refuses to loosen her grip on the wheel, and as a result it turns all the way over to an absurd degree.

SONJA: AAAAAAAAHHHHHHGgggggggg

HOWARD: Nooooooooo!

The hulking hull of the boat groans and creaks as it is hurled headlong onto the jagged alluvial rocks of the Gulf.

HOWARD: Nooooooooo!

The boat lurches, grunts, howls and splinters. Thousands of gallons of water splash up onto Howard and Sonja as they continue to struggle for control of the wheel. The lights fade.

SCENE 3.

Another longish pause in the darkness. The sounds of rupturing hull and rushing/crashing water become accompanied by the sounds of a rowdy Friday night crowd at a Crash Up Derby/Death Row Rodeo at a federal penitentiary somewhere between Dallas and Houston. Once again the side panels of the theater slide up into the ceilings, this time yielding up aluminum stadium bleachers filled with spectators. The audience is thus joined by great masses of new members and is treated to beer from vendors in large foam ten gallon hats in yellow and green. The rowdy crowd sounds are not from the high-tech sound apparatus anymore, which now blares Toby Keith and Shania Twain instead. We hear an ANNOUNCER's voice, and the sounds of many heavy American car engines revving maniacally and drilling themselves further and further into one another and into the dirt.

ANNOUNCER: Number nine. Number nine, you're out. Number nine, you're through. You are finished. Please exit the field. Number nine . . . That's you. This means you. Okay. And over on the other side here we've got about five of 'em workin on number twenty-three. I don't know what he did wrong . . .

While the announcer is speaking, Donnamarie appears onstage in a bright, bright follow spot. She dances as if someone who really meant a lot to her told her to perform a dance of 'unspeakable beauty.' She wears toe shoes.

ANNOUNCER: And he's out. Number twenty-three, this night's over for you, friend. Go ahead and step on out. Number nine you are OUT. You don't listen. Oh, my Lord . . . Well, what're you – where's your helmet? . . . You don't know. Boys, help him out of that vehicle. We've got a feisty number forty-two, ladies and gentlemen, comin around the outside and, HELLoe, he is not taking no for an answer over here on the near left side AND HE –

A huge crash is heard, the audience cries out in alarm and fascination. This is what they came for.

ANNOUNCER: Well, that is a MESS. Sixteen, the birthday party's over. Get on out. We'll need some attention from the fire department over here. Numbers sixteen and eleven. We are nearing the end of the fifth heat. Is this the last heat?

It soon becomes clear that she shares the stage with other figures. These are DOGS OR GOATS. They mill about the stage, visible only when they enter the follow spot. They behave unpredictably, and their numbers increase as her dance continues and becomes more and more exquisite. She compensates for them as necessary, but they do not wreck the splendor of the choreography.

The Announcer has now moved on to the Death Row Rodeo segment. It is unclear whether or not the crowd can see Donnamarie or the dogs. Probably they can not see her.

ANNOUNCER: Ladies and Gentlemen, most of these you see here tonight bulls average between one thousand and twelve hunnert pounds. We'd like to now introduce you to one bull tonight ladies and gentlemen – he's a monster. This here ol' boy weighs in twenny THREE hunnert pounds, ladies and gentlemen, *(the crowd reacts appropriately)* twenny three HUNNERT pounds of ugly and if you look to gate number eight. They call him the Boogieman, ladies and gentlemen and takin a ride to damnation tonight for your viewing pleasure – for your viewing PAIN – gate number eight, death row inmate Wallace P. Sanford ladies and gentlemen *(a louder buzzer sounds off, the sound of a metal gate opening on short notice and the crowd screams)* he's gonna try his luck! *(a short pause of twelve seconds, the crowd lets it loose)* TWELVE SECONDS! TWELVE – SECONDS, ladies and gentlemen! Now you tell me if you've ever seen anything like that in your life!

Donnamarie has completed her dance. The follow spot has faded and the lights, though they have come up slightly, remain terribly dim. She is focusing on getting all of the dogs offstage. When her task is finished, she confronts the audience.

DONNAMARIE: I met this woman one time and she read my horoscope. My mother used to cast horoscopes. She was some kind of a sensation in the fifties. She said "Ly – bra" instead of "Leebra." So when I was being born she said to the doctor, please can this baby be born in the next ten minutes or else it's going to be a Scorpio rising. And supposedly she wanted a Ly-bra rising, it's easier to get along with. The doctor agreed to do it, and told her to start pushing. She pushed too hard I guess? I don't know and something happened with the tubing. She ended up losing a lot of blood or whatever and fainting, and I ended up with Scorpio rising anyway. I guess then something happened with my father because I ended up going to live with another family that wasn't related. Anyway, this woman read my horoscope and told me that the Scorpio rising might be one of the reasons I have a hard time getting along with people. I told her she should really go fucking fuck herself. But I guess it makes sense. One time I had a boyfriend. He had a traditional family, we went to visit, we were lying in a hammock reading a-loud from this allsome book about a guy who gets really cranky with his family and can't figure out why. He has scary dreams, and something happens one night up at their country house – what is a country house? – and even they have company and the company notice it; it's in the night. So he goes to a hypnosis and finds out he's been abducted by aliens his whole life, and so was his dad, and so is his SON now – ! And there's all this lost time – he sits down to eat a t.v. dinner and then in the next moment, he doesn't even fall asleep, his t.v. dinner is cold and the t.v. is playing the star spangled banner! Remember that?! Now it's on all night with Half Pint and Pam Ewing selling face creams on the same show. Talking, sitting on couches – they're so nice to each other! Anyhow he had this aunt, this boyfriend I had had this aunt. And she was a couple sandwiches short of a picnic! I knew she could hear us and she was in a rocking chair farther down the porch and she started rocking faster and faster and turning her head around real sharp. I figured it was upsetting her so I kept on reading and reading and making comments. Later on when it was dinner time she kept on getting up and locking the door, the front door, probably sneaking out of the room and locking all the doors. She asked if she could close up the windows. They said, "Why, Maurene?" She said she was cold. She was a total liar. They got sick of her getting up and re-locking the front door a thousand times. They were onto her. She was the kind of woman who sits in the back seat and freaks out because she thinks you're running out of gas. She doesn't shut up about maybe we should pull over for some gas. They told her to knock it off. She made me sick that night. Not because of that but because we had this cream sauce on the salad and she had it all over her mouth when she took a drink from this nice wine glass. I kept looking at it and looking at it and finally I started gagging. I couldn't sit there with it so one of the times she got up to sneak around about the doors and the windows I did some sneaking of my own – I poured out whatever was in that glass and put it in the dishwasher! My boyfriend's mother saw me. She asked me what I was doing. I don't remember what I said but it was a lot better of an excuse than 'I'm cold' or 'it's cold in here' or whatever. Later on I found out that the family sent her to a community in Florida, and paid her rent for her and everything. And supposedly she stopped leaving the house. I wish I had her number. It would be so easy to prank her.

A broken down COWBOY limps onto the stage. He leans down and puts his hands on his knees and takes a few breaths to confirm that he is still living. The audience in the aluminum bleachers begins to collect whatever belongings it needs and exiting, not unnoisily, in streams. Most of its garbage is left behind on the bleachers, and janitors come out and clear it away.

DONNAMARIE: Well, how was it?

COWBOY: Didn't you see?

DONNAMARIE: Oh, yeah, I saw. I'm sorry you got hurt.

COWBOY: Where were you? I almost have to go to the hospital.

DONNAMARIE: I was here, I was here. But sometimes, I think once I got up to get something to eat. I kept on smelling the vinegar and the fried stuff. It was hard to pay attention.

COWBOY: It's like a fog comes over you sometimes, and you don't pay attention. I swear, woman I will never let you drive my car or my truck again.

DONNAMARIE: I thought I was doing better, I felt myself getting sharper but that cloud keeps coming back and covering me up, and it's almost always when I'm driving or in the grocery store. People's faces look all wrong, their expressions. I try not to look at them, I'm afraid they'll take some thing from me. Nothing out of my cart or anything like that but out of my soul. Like there's not that much left anyway. It was on sale maybe and everyone grabbed at it to try to save a buck. Buying something that wasn't even on their list in the first place. And the cloud just gets heavier and the next thing I know I'm calling people Fuckface just to wake up.

COWBOY: So in case you didn't notice I got really messed up out there. I think I broke a coupla ribs. But up here, by the sternum. I hope it didn't splinter and puncture my lung. It still could, ya know. I'm not outta the woods yet.

DONNAMARIE: I thought you said that if you can get up and walk away you were okay.

COWBOY: I said that when we were still in high school, maybe. I was riding for 4H then.

DONNAMARIE: Now what?

COWBOY: Now I'm older. And the only rodeos that are makin money are the ones against guys that are on death row anyway, so what do they care? They win the money cause they don't care. They're gonna be dead anyway.

DONNAMARIE: Maybe you better retire. You didn't used to care either.

COWBOY: Hell. Maybe you're right.

DONNAMARIE: I better go. I'm asking for trouble, this place is crawling with heat.

COWBOY: I need a ride.

DONNAMARIE: Well, I'm taking the bus.

COWBOY: You going home?

DONNAMARIE: I been sleeping in the cemetery. I have a sleeping bag there, a camp stove, and my pistol. It's pretty casual.

COWBOY: I need to see about these ribs. What if it rains?

DONNAMARIE: It hasn't rained. I like it. I feel cleaner than when I'm at home. If you sleep outside that's what happens.

COWBOY: You want to have a beer? I got some over with my stuff. They were in the cooler –

DONNAMARIE: I'll think it over. I feel like I want to be alone in the breeze at the cemetery, but I don't want to get there and then feel empty and there's no t.v. to turn on and I said no to beer. But I'm not taking you to the hospital so don't ask.

COWBOY: Am I allowed at the cemetery?

DONNAMARIE: No.

COWBOY: Oh.

DONNAMARIE: I know what happens. The fog lifts but only because there's nothing to cover.

COWBOY: Oh!

SCENE 4.

A dressing room. Sonja sits with her older half sister, MILCHA, a cabaret star. She is more Americanish than Sonja.

MILCHA: Honey let me tell you something. You're not like me. You need to have a man. It's alright. All kinds of people. But you've got to have a man and that's that. When you were a kid it was obvious – no one knew what to do with you or what to say – the problem was so obvious to everyone but you and you were only eight or nine or ten. It was a big relief when you grew up and started showing some womanhood. We all breathed a big sigh of relief and immediately you started dating. This man and that, taking indiscreet phone calls in restaurants and shopping in lingerie stores. I have to say though, I started to worry when I found out this one wasn't married.

SONJA: Milcha you're such a cunt.

MILCHA: I'm not either. Honestly, I know you better than you know yourself. I could be sitting here calling you a tramp or anything puritan like that. You're lucky, little kitten. We always recognized you for what you are and accepted you for only that. None of us ever gave you trouble about it, or guilt. *(One of Milcha's many chic alacritous ATTENDANTS enters with some papers and some gowns.)* You could have ended up with a family of people that expected you to stay with one man, or none, and who might disapprove if you didn't.

SONJA: *(indicating the attendant)* Do you mind?

MILCHA: What? They don't hear anything. I pay them not to. Isn't that right, Figgie?

FIGGIE: Beg pardon?

MILCHA: Right you are. *(Casts an I-told-you-so to Sonja)* What have you got there?

FIGGIE: It's some PR and the copies of the contract you wanted. And the gowns. They've just arrived.

MILCHA: Let me see. *(busying with the papers)* Kitten, I can't bear the thought of those gowns just now. Slip them on so I can look, will you?

SONJA: I'm afraid not, Milcha. You're too nasty today for favors. Positively abusive. And to think I came for a heart to heart chat –

MILCHA: Come on. I'm telling the truth. Don't you have that boyfriend coming to see the show tonight? You want me to look like some kind of shit? Hurry up, Sonja. I'm sorry if I offended you.

Sonja slips off her wrap dress and slips on one of the gowns to show Milcha. Milcha is now on the phone with her attorney as she browses the documents. She waves her hand in dismissal of one gown and Sonja begrudgingly slips it off and tries on another.

MILCHA: *(on the phone, as some more attendants enter with ice-filled washtubs of beverages and trays of fruit and finger sandwiches)* Well, I already signed it, Mor-tie. So what happens now? Well, what if I don't? Really, what can they do? And so what if we did go to the courts? What could happen? And then what would become of me? Would I go to hell? *(laughs)*. . . Alright. So you have your answer. *(rejects another gown, laughs into the phone)* Well, the truth is, Firm Favorite, that I'm available for breakfast tomorrow. But you'll have to be up early. I seriously doubt it. They're not even open at that hour. You'll have to come to my place. I'll cook. (*winks at Sonja*) Goodbye, Mor-tie. (*to Sonja*) I prefer the one with the peacock feathers.

SONJA: Great. You want it pressed?

MILCHA: Pressed. What century is that. Where's Figgie? It needs to be steamed. Listen, Kitten. I've got to warm up my voce. Make tracks, will you? Unless you want a finger sandwich –

SONJA: No, I had better go meet Howard. I think we won't stay for the show tonight after it all.

MILCHA: Ah, revenge. A dish best served cold, didn't you know? I guess not. Suit yourself. These are the greatest songs I've ever written.* Hit it, Figgie.

Figgie enters quickly and begins playing the modest upright in the corner of the dressing room. Milcha joins in lustily.

MILCHA: (*singing*) "Lights out tonight, trouble in the heartland Got a head-on collision smashin' in my guts, man I'm caught in a crossfire that I don't understand. But there's one thing I know for sure, girl I don't give a damn for the same old played-out scenes

And I don't give a damn for just the in-betweens Honey I want the heart, I want the soul, I want control right now You better listen to me baby – "

She grips Sonja by the shoulders and sings the remainder of the song to her face, as if she's making it up on the spot, but with her eyes closed.

"Workin' in the fields till you get your back burned Workin' neath the wheel till you get your facts learned Honey I got my facts learned real good right now You better get it straight darling Poor man wanna be rich Rich man wanna be king And a king ain't satisfied till he rules everything I wanna go out tonight, I wanna find out what I got For the ones who had a notion and a notion deep inside That it ain't no sin to be glad you're alive I wanna find one face that ain't lookin' through me I wanna find one place I wanna spit in the face of these Badlands

You gotta live it every day, let the broken hearts stand For the price you gotta pay Keep pushin' till it's understood and these Badlands start treatin' us good . . ."

Figgie wastes no time seguing into the next number. GARRY, another attendant, turns the pages of the arrangement for him.

"I've got a sixty nine chevy with a three ninety six, fuelie heads and a hearst on the floor . . ."

Sonja gathers her purse and wrap and makes for the door.

"She's waiting tonight down in the parking lot, outside the seven eleven store . . ."

Sonja puts her hand on the doorknob but lacks the strength to turn it.

"Me and my partner, Sonny, built her straight out of scratch and he rides with me from town to town . . ."

Slowly, almost imperceptibly, Sonja's forehead comes to rest on the door.

"We only run 'em for the money, got no strings attached. We shut 'em up and then we shut 'em down . . ."

The lights fade but Milcha's song continues, as

SCENE 5.

Lacey is coming home from yet another hard day at work. She lives in an apartment complex that was built in the mid nineteen seventies. Her door is a robust orange color and the carpets are light in color and the furniture is all rush and caning with cushions. There is a window-like opening between the kitchen and living area and there are three stools. There are also replicas of rare and exotic plants throughout the apartment. Two sliding glass doors lead onto a concrete balcony. Lacey sadly puts her bag down on one of the chairs at the small dinette set, and deposits her mail in a pile on the table. She hangs her keys on a little hook by the door. She sighs heavily, and confronts the audience.

LACEY: I wasn't always a nurse. I used to be a flight attendant. I worked for Eastern Airlines, back in the heyday, way before they ever thought it would be possible that they would ever fold. *(She heaves another sigh.)* I was tall and thin then. I was like a reed of sea-grass. That was when I first got this apartment. Back then it was a pretty glamorous little place to live. I even had an affair with one of the pilots. You won't believe me when I tell you that they used to measure the circumference of our thighs. Once a month. If you were more than seventeen inches twice in a row they fired you. Pretty daunting, but I was young and I didn't worry about that kind of thing. A lot of things were different then. There used to be a diving board at the pool back then, and there were parties and the whole complex would go. People were more into earthy crafts and pottery, but their lives were not earthy. Our lives were more airy-fairy, unserious, perhaps insufficiently careful. I enjoyed myself, everyone made sure they did things that they enjoyed. Whatever your ‘thing’ was, that was what you did and no one questioned you. I won’t make a comparison to now. I know I’m stuck. But recently I went to a place that had been a camp. And it was so great. The bathrooms and the rooms were not finished off, but the structure of two by fours inside the places were exposed, so you could see the homemade handiwork, you got the feeling that they had been built by one very adept carpenter over a period of time. And the two by fours were painted white. Even in the bathrooms and showers. There were corners and shelves built in, for soap or for toilet paper or what not. It was nice. Very practical, and comforting. You didn’t examine things to make sure they were clean. It didn’t matter as much. Because there was still care put in. The walls themselves were painted bright, strong blue. Which you appreciated especially at night. Just a light bulb in the ceiling with a beaded metal pull cord. It felt like childhood, it felt like someone had cared. And it was a privilege to be there, to spend time there. I hope I never forget it. Instead of roaches and rats, there were spiders and deer curled up out back in the woods in the sunshine. *(She sighs.)* There aren’t roaches and rats here. Sometimes I imagine that there’s more to this apartment. I see different hallways that lead to different rooms, with wallpaper, almost Victorian era, and none of these rooms have wallpaper. Maybe a loft space, maybe something more contemporary, with a yard somehow, an old yard with green grass that is fine and cool and stone walls and children running around, nice children, not like what I see these days, and families, and rickety old iron gates. Private and friendly. Plants in heavy white plaster potters. People hiding in their houses and you finally get to go in and see them, and talk to them.

Chances are they're out of practice and don't know how. But sometimes that's better. It's not as exhausting.

The doorbell rings. She answers it. It's Howard. He looks around to see if anything's changed since the last time he was here.

LACEY: When was the last time you were here?

HOWARD: Either when you were sick, or when you had people over for a meeting. It looks nice.

He sits down.

HOWARD: I think Mary might come over too. I think she might be interested.

LACEY: Mary, Mary, Mary. Let me get changed. Do you know where everything is in case you want something to drink or something?

HOWARD: I'll just wait until you're back.

Lacey goes to change. Howard makes an effort to hang out and cracks his knuckles. He looks around the apartment, looks at Lacey's mail, but becomes ashamed a little and looks steadily at the floor in front of his chair. As he stares his sense of shame becomes gradually overwhelming. By the time Lacey returns in her around-the-house clothes, he is in tears.

LACEY: Howard! Jesus, what is it!

Howard shakes his head and covers his eyes, tighter, tighter! He is ashamed to show anyone his shame, let alone one of his subordinates from work. Lacey, wanting to fix it, wanting to find out what is wrong, tries to pry his hands from his eyes.

LACEY: Come on, Howard! Oh, Howard! Howard! Jesus!

It is so upsetting and frustrating and unexplainable that Lacey starts crying too. She gives up trying to pry his hands from his eyes and starts slapping Howard in exasperation and boxes his ears. He falls off his chair onto the carpet. He cries and cries, sobbing now, in pain, and Lacey, feeling instantly horribly guilty, covers her own face and cries very hard.

LACEY: Oh, my God! Oh, my God, I don't know why I did that! Why did I do that? Why! Why! Oh, my God!

Not knowing what else to do, she launches around the room in tight circles, bellowing and crying.

LACEY: Oh, God forgive me! I didn't mean it! I don't know why I did it! I don't know why! I don't know why! I don't know why I DID that! *(she sobs and sobs and tries to scream)* Why! Why! Why! Oh, God! God help me! God forgive me!

She cries and sobs and runs around and around. Howard cries more softly, curled into a ball on his side.

LACEY: I'm sorry. I'm so sorry Howard. I guess I didn't know what else to do.

She kneels down by Howard and pulls him up onto her, encircling him with her arms. It seems to help, and they stay that way for a long time. A tiny trickle of blood runs slowly out of each of Howard's ears. The doorbell rings.

HOWARD: That must be Mary.

LACEY: Mary? Is that you?

SONJA: No. It's Sonja. Howard's girlfriend.

LACEY: Sonja?

Sonja enters.

LACEY: I'm afraid I've done something terrible. Something terrible and violent in just an instant, before I even knew what I was doing. I feel awful. I think he's okay, but that's no excuse. Sonja, Howard's my boss. And I trust him. I don't know why I did this. I boxed his ears.

HOWARD: I was having a hard time to begin with. But I didn't know it. I didn't know it until I got here and you went to go get changed. It just became so quiet in here.

SONJA: What should I do? Do you want me to leave? Is this a crime or an emergency? Should I call the police?

LACEY: I might feel better if you called the police and pressed charges. I feel terribly, terribly guilty.

HOWARD: Lacey, I feel guilty too. I feel like I'm just as guilty as you. Like I provoked you. I didn't know I was provoking you to violence, but apparently I was. What's strange is, I feel very, very close to you right now. I'm shivering. Sonja.

LACEY: Sonja, I don't know what to tell you to do. Maybe we should wait until Mary gets here.

SONJA: Maybe she could help us define it. Maybe I should sit down. Or should I leave?

HOWARD: I don't want you to leave.

LACEY: Would you mind sitting on the floor with us? It's clean.

SONJA: Okay.

LACEY: Sonja, I'm so sorry. I've never been a violent type person. And I don't want to make excuses about this.

HOWARD: You mean about that woman last week?

LACEY: I don't want to say that she is why this happened. I have a strong feeling that that would be a cop-out.

SONJA: I hate talks about responsibility. Sometimes things like this happen. And they happen very quickly, Lacey. I was always afraid of heights and I never knew why. But the reason is because when I'm up high, all I can think about is how easy it would be to jump right off, before I even know what I'm doing. My sister has the same weakness, and she is a different type of person altogether from me. You want me to call the police on you perhaps because you're afraid. You've discovered a new part of yourself and you don't know what to do. But how often do we discover a new part of ourself?

A knock at the door.

LACEY: Mary? Come in.

MARY enters slowly and assuredly.

LACEY: Mary. I don't know what else to say except things aren't the same as they were when we spoke on the phone. I've slapped Howard and boxed his ears and we're trying to figure out what to do.

SONJA: We could use your input.

MARY: What have you done about it so far?

HOWARD: We're talking about it.

MARY: That's the best thing you can do.

LACEY: But don't you think we better call the police or something?

MARY: How do you feel about it HOWARD?

HOWARD: I feel a lot better. I mean, I feel better than I did before I came here today. I've been feeling pretty bad lately.

SONJA: We crashed our boat last week.

MARY: Oh, I'm sorry. Was it traumatic?

SONJA: It was violent in its own way – we could have drowned – and we were fighting. Howard said some pretty terrible things to me.

MARY: Is that true, Howard?

HOWARD: I think we both said terrible things.

LACEY: I had a violent encounter last week also. We were talking about that possibility, but I think my actions stand alone.

MARY: Then I'll call the police. *(moving toward the phone)* Sonja, I'm doing an interview with Milcha later over drinks.

SONJA: That's great. Good for both your careers.

MARY: Sure.

HOWARD: Listen, Mary, do you think we could get by without the police here? I'm ringing a little but otherwise I'm fine. I actually feel a lot lighter. I don't know if I want that kind of interpretation, you know?

MARY: Lacey, do you feel like you've committed a crime?

LACEY: Yes. But it's a crime against humanity, through Howard. Not a crime against Howard. I don't feel like local law enforcement is adequate.

MARY: Who do I call for that?

LACEY: Now I think I should see a clergyman instead.

SONJA: Maybe we should just forget the whole thing. Lacey, you'll want to forget when tomorrow comes.

MARY: I'm leaving then.

HOWARD: We'll never forget it.

LACEY: Mary, I'd rather you didn't leave. We need an objective.

SONJA: Howard, I brought my car. If you'd like a ride . . . we could go somewhere, talk . . .

HOWARD: Lacey? Are you alright to be left by yourself?

SONJA: She could come with us, too, if she wants, if you want . . .

LACEY: That's very kind, Sonja, but I feel I've intruded already.

SONJA: I'm also thinking of Howard. He's not going to be able to look you in the face at work if we leave now without you.

LACEY: I might not be at work. Maybe it's time for a change.

Piano music begins to play. Sonja and Lacey and Howard each share a long hug. Mary has left, and Sonja and Howard file out now leaving Lacey alone. Lacey sits for a moment, and then goes to one of her closets and begins cleaning it out. The lights fade, and the piano music takes over, picks up and is joined by many other instruments. The music swells.

SCENE 6.

The aluminum bleachers have long since vanished and are now replaced by elegant banquettes and tables with dim lampettes in the middle. New fans augment the current audience, but these are different from the Crash Up Derby/Rodeo crowd. Mostly male and very urbane, they soak up and respond devotedly to the entertainment, ordering drinks from nicely turned out waiters with silver trays. Milcha is in the heat of her third encore. She is backed by a sizable orchestra.

MILCHA: *(singing)* "Well, I'm ridin' down Kingsley, figuring I'll get a drink I've got the radio up loud so I don't have to think And I take her to the floor, looking for a moment when the world seems right And I tear in to the guts oh oh oh oh oh Of Something in the night. Well, we're born with nothin' and better off that way As soon as you've got somethin' they send someone to try and take it away You can ride this road till dawn without another human being in sight

It's just kids wasted on oh oh oh oh oh Somethin' in the night. And nothin' is forgotten or forgiven when it's your last time around And I've got stuff runnin' round my head That I just can't live down When we found the things we loved, They were crushed and dying in the dirt.

We tried to pick up the pieces, And get away without getting hurt, But they caught us at the state line, And burned our cars in one last fight, And left us running burned and blind, Chasing something in the night."

She keeps singing, hitting all the notes and thrilling the audience. When this song is over, they cry for more and more. She gives it to them. She sings more songs.

MILCHA: Ah, the night Figgie.

FIGGIE: Yes, the night. What is it about that night, Milcha?

MILCHA: Well, it's cold in the night.

FIGGIE: Yes . . .

MILCHA: And it's LONELY that night –

FIGGIE: Yes, but what ELSE?

MILCHA: Now just what are you trying to tell me, Figgie? *(then recognizing the opening chords)* Oh, NOW I see what you're getting at! *(sings)* "Well, they're still racin' out at the trestles but that blood it never burned in her veins Now I hear she's got a house up in Fairview And a style she's tryin' to maintain Well, if she wants to see me You can tell her that I'm easily found Tell her there's a spot out 'neath Abrams bridge and tell her There's a darkness on the edge of town There's a darkness on the e-e-e-e-e-dge of town Well everybody's got a secret, sonny" (even YOU, Figgie!)

"Somethin' that they just can't face" (watch it, Garry!)

"Some people spend their whole lives tryin' to keep it They carry it with 'em every step that they take Till someday they just cut it loose Cut it loose or let it drag 'em down Well no one asks you any questions or looks to long in your face In the darkness on the edge of town In the darkness on the e-e-e-e-edge of town"

She is a tough and no-nonsense performer, bringing her adoring fans back to their roots, roots they never even knew they had.

"Well some folks are born into the good life And other folks get it any way they know how

Me, I lost my money and I lost my wife Them things don't seem to matter much to me now.

Tonight I'll be on that hill Cause I can't stop I'll be on that hill with everything I got There's lives on the line where dreams are found and lost I'll be there on time and I'll pay the cost

For wantin' things that can only be found In the darkness on the edge of town In the darkness on the e-e-e-e-e-e-e-e-e-e-e-e – "

She is temporarily stuck on the note whilst Figgie rifles frantically through the sheet music for the transition into the next song.

FIGGIE: *(shouting over the cacophony)* How do we get out of this one, darling, do you remember?

Still drilling the note and running out of breath fast, Milcha indicates with her body language that she has no earthly idea.

FIGGIE: I KNOW I had it here somewhere . . .

At last Figgie finds it and bangs out the opening chords of the next song.

MILCHA: Ah! Now that's out of the frying pan and into the fire, Figgie! Well, I'm too tired for that one! I can't! I just can't!

FIGGIE: You can do it Milcha! They're BEGGING! They're DESPERATE for you out there!

MILCHA: Damn you, Figggggiiiiiieeee! *(madly sings and dances, in spite of herself)* "On a rattlesnake speedway in the Utah desert I pick up my money and head back into town

Ridin' cross the Waynesboro county line I've got my radio on and I'm just killin' time Workin' all day in my daddy's garage Drivin' all night chasin' some mirage Pretty soon little girl I'm gonna take charge Well, the dogs on main street howl cause they understand If I could take one moment into my hands Mister I ain't a boy No, I'm a man And I believe in the Promised Land Buddy, I've done my best to live the right way I get up every morning and go to work each day But your eyes go blind and your blood runs cold Sometimes I feel so weak I just want to explode Explode and tear this whole town apart Take a knife and cut this pain from my heart Find somebody itchin' for somethin' to start Well the dogs on main street howl cause they understand If I could take one moment into my hands Mister I ain't a boy No, I'm a man And I believe in the Promised Land There's a dark cloud risin' from the desert floor I've packed my bags and I'm headed straight into the storm Gonna be twister to blow everything down That ain't got the faith to stand its ground Blow away the dreams that tear you apart

Blow away the dreams that break your heart Blow away the lies that leave you nothin' but lost and brokenhearted Well the dogs on main street howl cause they understand If I could take one moment into my hands Mister I ain't a boy No, I'm a man And I believe in the Promised Land Yes, I believe in the Promised Land."

She performs a support-the-troops dance sequence.

I believe! I believe in it! Who doubts it! Who DARES! I believe! Support the troops! Bring 'em home! I believe! I believe we should support the troops! Bring 'em home . . .

Eventually she collapses in exhaustion, yet not before the audience starts to really worry. She is perspiring and spent, yet somehow continuing to salute the troops. Figgie and Garry do not notice at first and continue playing, turning pages and singing back-up furiously, then upon seeing her push the piano neatly back into place and rush to her aid.

FIGGIE: No. No. No. No. Sh. Shh. No no no no.

SCENE 6A.

Backstage Figgie applies a towel, a heavy bathrobe and a bottle of Evian with a red nipple on top. Milcha drops her soaking gown and gives herself over to the care of Figgie, Garry and two other attendants. She collapses gracefully into a tall director's chair and nurses quietly on the bottle. They remove her headpiece and towel Milcha's scalp and forehead. They clean the insides of Milcha's ears with a hot washcloth and elevate her feet, wrapping them in herbally-treated buntings. Once Milcha has finished her bottle Figgie brings icepacks for her throat and a steaming hot beverage for her to sip at the same time. A hospital gurney made up with white sheets and pillows is wheeled up next to the director's chair. Milcha obediently crawls onto it and collapses once again, opening the back of her robe for the attendants to begin massaging her roughly about the buttocks. Mary enters. She has a backstage pass hanging around her neck.

MARY: Milcha, it was an excellent performance. I'm Mary Oliver. We spoke over the phone.

MILCHA: *(weakly)* Mary, how do you do. They're about to wheel me away. I've got to have an enema and then I should be better able to talk with you. You see, I'm completely spent.

Figgie will show you to my dressing room. Please make yourself at home there and I'll join you in about an hour.

MARY: *(looking at her watch)* Well – All right, certainly.

The gurney is wheeled away as Figgie whisks Mary firmly to the dressing room.

SCENE 7.

A fog descends on the empty backstage area. Soon nothing is visible but a grey mist, which hangs in the air and then seems to settle into what now is the earth. It is the cemetery. The Cowboy is making out with Donnamarie in a way that is uncomfortable. Farther along stand two STATUES OF COWBOYS, LARGE and SMALL. The Small one can move and talk, the Large one can also but won't.

SMALL COWBOY STATUE: I ain't been to town for quite an age. Tho' I reckon this town don't look like much, plenty a buildens, plenty a folk. No place to git any provisions or vittles, no one friendly enough to invite y'in for some grub an they send the sheriff out after ye 'f they see y' fixin to make a campfire. Walk out five miles on foot for a banker boy's whisky an no kind word. Plenty a green grass an no horses to munch it.

Yeah, it's lonely to be a cowhand, you know it? Hey? I know they always say that but unless you're REALLY busy, no matter where you are, you can't help but end up looken out into the distance far, far ahead of you and all around you. Looken and LOOKen. I reckon I need m' space, but once you start in to all that looken. I sometimes can git lonely jess looken downward toward the grass or at some lowly insects on the earth.

I feel like I want somethen then, like I want someone to come along and help me – Sometimes I'm jess desperate an I cry out, 'I'll take anyone for a friend! Just come along! Just appear to me!' 'Hurry!'

Hey! Hey! You're comen around, now! O-K Corral!

LARGE COWBOY STATUE: Heh, heh, heh!

SMALL COWBOY STATUE: Dang, m' leg! Y' really put a hurten on it, it's a-blee –

LARGE COWBOY STATUE: Sun's in m' eyes. I'll take yer hat, partner, you don't mind. Got any chaw? I sure could use it, boy, thank ye. Heh he!

I don't want any friends. They won't know how to treat me. How to touch me. And if I have a friend, I'll need to be touched. And in the right way! Don't just jab at me, friend, GRIP me. Keep it on there nice and firm. Careful not to tickle me. Don't tickle m' hide by stroken too lightly, and don't vex m' flesh muscle-meat by a lot of un-introducted jabben/grabben. And don't call me on the phone. If you want to see me, come over – just give me a holler when you see me. Once you find me, don't ask me a lot of questions. Don't PROBE me. Cain't STAND proben! But don't be uninterested in what I'm tellen you either. And it's okay to jess sit without talken.

I've had a friend come along, try to find SOLUTIONS to m' problems instead of just listenen to me complain. They'd end up lecturen me, tryen to boss me or tell me what I SHOULD do. I SHOULD look at it different, I SHOULD take some sort of action agin m' problems, I SHOULD go to a church or stop thinken about m'self s' much, to start to thinken of others. Don' tell me what to do. Ye're not too much help, now are ye? You ought not to just stand there, like ye're taunten me. Like, like as if you're sayen 'Okay, well, I'm not even gonna try, because I'll just do the wrong thing' like telling me that I'm touchy or persnickety without comen out and sayen it altogether. Well, believe me, I read you loud and clear, m' friend.

That's all right. Well, that's all right. You jess stand there taken up the space here, not sayen a word.

Glad I don't have m'horse here after all – he'd be like to break his leg on these stones all over. To tell the truth, knowen that people are always like that in the end doesn't make me any the less lonely-feelen sometimes, like you said.

Come on, whaddya say we sing us a song as long as we cain't drink and we cain't build us a fire? Come on Git along, little doggie, get a long – Hey you ain't singin! All right then. Well, all right whaddya say you pony on up with me an sidle out to that mean highway strip an git a taste a that sad happy hour whisky an impolite conversation? No? Well, who needs you, boy? I got plenty a time to waste somewheres else. C'mon! I don't like you either but maybe we can find some girls! It's hard when you're by yourself! They don't trust you as easy! An I can never say the right thing. C'mon! Please? I don't want to say the wrong thing! I don't want to say it wrong.

DONNAMARIE: I really need to get back to basics.

COWBOY: The basics of love?

DONNAMARIE: I'm talken about the spiritual here, the basic physical.

COWBOY: That's what I'm talken about too.

DONNAMARIE: What about kill or be killed?

COWBOY: Yeah?

DONNAMARIE: Yeah. I just thought of it. And it could be right here, starting with us.

SCENE 8.

Mary lounges alone in Milcha's dressing room as if she had been here a long time. She speaks into a handheld recorder.

MARY: If the windows are closed, you will never hear the soughing of the trees. You circle them, and their breath encircles you. What is the tree dreaming?

End

**Milcha did not actually write any of her songs. They are plagiarized here from the "Darkness on the Edge of Town" album by Bruce Springsteen ©1978.*

THE
LOST ACTS
OF
CRIME OR EMERGENCY

ACT X

SCENE 1.

A woman we've known previously as DONNAMARIE stands with a clipboard in a vast field of swollen roadkill deer, all terribly mangled into impossible postures. She wears the work uniform of the Dallas/Fort Worth D.O.T. One of her own arms is terribly swollen.

Something makes the bodies of the deer seem non-present, as if they are projections . . .

. . . Psychological projections. Donnamarie examines one carcass in particular, an exceptionally unmangled one.

DONNAMARIE: I'm getting used to it out here, seeing them all messed up. The guts. My brother? Oh my God. He used to always have to pull over and mess around with them. Maybe that's why I end up I don't care about it. Even the smell. It's just bodies. He used to take out leg bones and put them in the backs of my dolls saying they needed spinal cords, stuff like that. Well, he was kind of my brother, sort of by blood, but not really. He was vile. Like a villain, but I was always laughing till I shit my pants I couldn't even help it. *(Pause.)* If you think about it now, you can plainly see he was really creative. *(Pause.)* This is the time of day I always think of Keith, no matter what.

She looks at the sky and then rolls the unmangled deer carcass onto its back. Its hind legs fall open.

DONNAMARIE: *(cont'd)* Oh, Keith. You were the love of my life. We never thought a tornado would hit us, and so it never did. But we knew that one day we would get pulled over by the cops, and you hated me cause I looked into that state trooper's brown, brown eyes. Hey. I'm sorry . . . telling him that I was scared of the construction trucks, that I had to go to the bathroom, and keeping my hands folded on my lap just like if I was at a church and had white gloves on.

She begins lightly dragging her swollen hand and fingers across its groin. Not its genitals, just the place where the leg meets the abdomen. The fluid in her arm rushes all at once down to her fingertips, causing her a certain amount of pain.

DONNAMARIE: *(cont'd)* Ow, it hurts it to bend over like that.

She stands looking hatefully at her swollen arm for a moment. Unbelievably, the deer disappear and the field becomes just an expansive lawn, the same as the cemetery without the gravestones. Donnamarie lies down and holds her swollen arm above her to give her fingers a break. Then, with plant-like intelligence, hundreds of stones can be heard breaking through the ground and pushing their way up through the dirt where the graves would be. They are rough, unhewn hunks of granite and marble in their natural state before they were cut into grave markers.

DONNAMARIE: *(referring to the deer/stones)* I don't know how they do it, but they tell me I'm alive and I have a fucking right to be here if I wanna be, you know.

She rests. Dappled sunlight, an exquisite afternoon. Unbeknownst to Donnamarie, a man we may or may not recognize as HOWARD strolls among the uncut stones many rows away here at the cemetery. He alights on one. He is alone.

HOWARD: I am sitting on top of this stone and it is underneath. *(Pause.)* Or. *(Pause.)* I am fixed here in the grass and he, the stone, is sitting on top of me. *(Pause.)* Am I the one who is sitting on the stone, or am I the stone on which HE is sitting?

The question perplexes him.

He stands up, wondering who is what now. The answer remains totally unclear, and his uncertainty is accompanied by a feeling of curious and fascinating darkness.

HOWARD: *(cont'd)* I can't doubt that this stone stands in some secret relationship to me.

He sits for hours, fascinated by the puzzle it sets before him. Finally,

HOWARD: *(cont'd)* This is eternal. Time does not move here. If I stay, I lose hold of my future, permanently.

A COWBOY enters who is vaguely familiar to us, but unknown to Howard. He is looking for Donnamarie. He carries a cat carrier, a plastic litter box scooper and a six pack of beer.

COWBOY: Where is she?

Howard, lost in strange, rapturous thought, doesn't answer.

COWBOY: Hey. You. Are you a pervert? What did you do? Did you do somethin? Hey what's the matter with you now. Are you messed up?

Howard, sensing a formal presence on both sides of his current reality, turns his head and his unseeing eyes slowly toward the Cowboy.

HOWARD: My childhood . . . hhhhhhhhhhhhhu . . .

The cat yowls suddenly from inside its carrier, startling the Cowboy badly.

He almost drops everything, then thinks maybe he should put it all down anyway so he can punch Howard.

COWBOY: I'm'na punch you, you weirdo!

Instead, too unnerved, he lurches off to find Donnamarie. Howard's unseeing eyes are searching avidly for something: something unseen.

SCENE 2.

A luxuriously appointed rehearsal studio belonging to a cabaret singer known to us and the world as MILCHA.

Enter FIGGIE, assistant, accompanist and accomplice to Milcha. The doorbell is ringing.

Figgie admits PAUL PIANO TUNER, who enters, red and sweating, with a special tool bag.

He goes straight to the piano and sets his bag down. Wipes his forehead. He plays some notes. A grimace spreads across his face. He looks under the hood. Turns to Figgie.

PAUL PIANO TUNER: Look, if this is like bone cancer we're looking at here I'm going to have to leave and come back again with the heavy artillery.

FIGGIE: Well, it has been a long time. It's overdue.

PAUL PIANO TUNER: Yeh. I'll say. Hey uh, how about a glass of cold water?

FIGGIE: Sure. Of course. Do you want coffee?

PAUL PIANO TUNER: Uhhhh –

FIGGIE: Like an iced espresso or something?

PAUL PIANO TUNER: Yeah . . . YEAH! *(laughs with bewildered delight)* That would be GREAT!

Figgie exits. Paul Piano Tuner sets to work, grunting and sweating, grimacing, but with new inspiration. Figgie returns with ice water and iced espresso for Paul Piano Tuner.

PAUL PIANO TUNER: Aw, you really UNDERSTAND!

Enthusiastic, nodding sips. Then he sets back to work.

FIGGIE: Just let me know if you need anything else.

Closing some French doors in a gingerly way that tells us someone is on the other side of them, Figgie exits. Paul Piano Tuner continues working. After a little while SONJA enters meekly through those same French doors. She's been sleeping in the next room but now is getting ready to go somewhere.

PAUL PIANO TUNER: *(looking up at her in amazement)* I didn't know anybody was in there! . . . hi!

SONJA: Oh, it was me. I'm just going somewhere.

PAUL PIANO TUNER: *(agape)* May I know your name? And I'm Paul. I didn't even know anyone else was in there. You're a vision. I . . . I feel like mortally wounded!

SONJA: My name is Sonja. Where did you get that iced coffee?

PAUL PIANO TUNER: Uh, from the assistant.

SONJA: Oh. Okay.

PAUL PIANO TUNER: *(holding it out to her)* Unh, do you want some?

Pause.

SONJA: This is my sister's place. My sister is the owner of this.

She exits. Paul Piano Tuner, still holding out his coffee in a gesture of unbidden offering, doesn't know whether to take a drink from it himself now or not. He sets it down warily and looks at it. Then he looks at the piano again for a few minutes. The phone rings. When the answering machine picks up, it's a message from the

LARGE COWBOY STATUE, for Sonja. His accent is different, but the voice is unmistakable from ACT I.

LARGE COWBOY STATUE: *(from the answering machine)* Hey, Sonja! I think this is still the right number. How are you, honey? Well, I just keep thinking of you and I had to figure out why and I – it's because it's uh, it's June . . . June is uh when the ROSES blossom. And I think of you when the roses really start to look just so extra gorgeous and plentiful, like more than you could ever ah, imagine . . . and um, that's kind of the, impression you made on me when your – when I first got to know you, and it's a lasting impression . . . And I hope you're doing good it's a beautiful, June. It's one of the prettiest Junes I can remember. Because the weather has been so gray and cold. It's been actually a cold . . . June. And it's extraordinary. And the trees all seem to be like super fresh. They have they seem to be uh extending their time of – youth – into adulthood. They're still, they're adults but they have the tender fresh vulnerable leaves – that are easily chewed by insects. But there's just enough there's so much of everything that it doesn't matter. They can lose they can lose as much leaves as they want there's plenty to go around. Anyway. *(Pause.)* Love you, Sonja. I'll be talking to you. Bye, baby.

After a moment:

PAUL PIANO TUNER: *(thinking out loud)* I feel like I need to do something irrevocable. Like smash this piano. I know exactly how to do it too. I know exactly how to smash a fucking piano. And don't think I haven't thought about doing it before either!

He resumes tuning, fevered and bothered.

PAUL PIANO TUNER: Yeah. I could smash this piano up. What would she think of me THEN . . .

Continues tuning, forgets the idea of smashing the piano since something isn't working right with it – no point in smashing up an imperfect piano. Realizes he needs another tool.

PAUL PIANO TUNER: I'm'na come back with the other tools.

Starts packing up. Stops because he thinks of something, then

PAUL PIANO TUNER: Aw, I should really just come back with the right tools.

He resumes packing the tools again, this time at a much slower pace and with an occasional, thoughtful glance at the piano.

SCENE 3.

We see Lacey is at home in her apartment. She is in her kitchen, examining the contents of her refrigerator. She is confused.

LACEY: Something's wrong. This mayonnaise should go in the door! Why would I of put it there? What's the matter with me!

She huffily puts the item back where it belongs: in the door. She checks a few freshness-dates (she figures as long as she's here. . .), and throws some things into the garbage.

Then she begins rubbing her eyes and temples.

She decides to try to make her hair into French braids to pick up her spirits, but fails repeatedly throughout the following scene.

SCENE 3A.

In a different apartment in another part of town. SEAN CROSBY with two other men probably of his same family. Together, they make a MAN FAMILY.

Sean has some salve that has to be applied to his burns which he acquired in a different play laying on a hot parking lot due to a mistake in medication for a different medical issue.

He has to ask one of the other two men to do it for him, since he can't reach all of the burned areas. It's emotionally awkward for the other man to do it, but physically awkward for Sean to do it. The other man's name is RICHIE, and perhaps they are brothers or brothers-in-law. Richie loves Sean, and wants to help him – it's just awkward. Once his hesitation becomes more awkward than the situation itself, he agrees to do it.

The third member of the man family, PRESTON, gets a bowl of cereal as men will do late at night when they live together with other men. He watches the other two as he eats. This is the status quo for a couple of minutes.

PRESTON: It's a predicament from where I'm sitting. You know you owe me all that money I fronted you for those payments, Richie.

Richie grunts.

PRESTON: Did you ever call the Social Security office?

RICHIE: Nah. Haven't had the chance. It's closed a lot of the time.

PRESTON: You better take care of that. It'll come back on you one day.

They continue to speak in non-theatrical words and tones not fully audible to the audience. Sean is no longer hearing them. He is enjoying the application of the salve because Richie is so gentle about it.

SCENE 3B.

The sun has risen in a near-apocalyptic way at the cemetery. Easter eggs are hidden among the tufts of grass around the graves. Children turned out in ribbons and bonnets and short pants and suspenders filter in, searching and locating, and filling up their little baskets with them.

The scene with Sean Crosby continues, but the scene with Lacey ends.

Howard is gone but Donnamarie is up and about. She is dealing with a cat's dirty litter box and wears knee socks and a nightgown. Her arm is still dreadfully swollen. The ground is littered with some paper plates and plastic cups and beer bottles. Used paper napkin balls are stiff and orange with dried barbecue sauce wipings. The Cowboy sleeps in an old sleeping bag nearby. A STATE TROOPER enters with a letter on dainty stationery.

DONNAMARIE: You found me. You fucker.

STATE TROOPER: I got your note –

DONNAMARIE: I always knew you'd find me.

STATE TROOPER: – but it's not appropriate.

DONNAMARIE: But, was I wrong to mind my goddamn feelings? Even if it's this kind of payback?

STATE TROOPER: I'm sorry, I don't even know. I'm on duty.

DONNAMARIE: Yeah, but you can still . . . Do you even remember pulling me over?

STATE TROOPER: Yes.

DONNAMARIE: Did you know who it was when you got my note?

STATE TROOPER: I remembered that your car was filthy. And I was mad at myself later for asking for an updated registration even though the one you handed me was not expired yet. And when I asked you if you knew that you were speeding you told me you thought it might be because you had ants in your pants. You said you had to go to the bathroom.

DONNAMARIE: Yeah so you remembered. You did remember me.

STATE TROOPER: I knew the passenger in the vehicle with you was carrying a concealed weapon.

DONNAMARIE: So why did you let us go.

STATE TROOPER: I did let you go.

DONNAMARIE: I KNOW!

Pause

DONNAMARIE: That passenger was my brother. Keith.

She folds her hands in front of her heart.

DONNAMARIE: (cont'd) Yeah. And he's not even alive anymore. And you saw him. That passenger was my brother. And you saw him. You saw a DEAD man!

STATE TROOPER: No.

DONNAMARIE: Yeah. Yeah. A DEAD man.

STATE TROOPER: I said no.

DONNAMARIE: I wanna go out to a restaurant with you. COME ON! You could tell me how you think I can make my life better. You can tell me, tell me, tell me about your Dad, the piano lessons or whatever. You're so young! I wanna feel sorry for you. COME ON!!

STATE TROOPER: I can't. I'm on duty.

Then the first few bars of The Entertainer being played on a piano. Fades.

STATE TROOPER: . . . I don't want you to see me without my uniform.

DONNAMARIE: Okay, "Please."

STATE TROOPER: Please. Please just leave it where it is.

DONNAMARIE: I saw you coming up behind us and I knew it was me you were looking for. You were riding in my blind spot on purpose and I knew you could see me trying to find you in one or the other of the mirrors. I could feel you guiding me over to that all-the-way-right lane, even though I did it myself. I waited for you to put your lights on, but you waited to put them on until the very last possible second and I loved how it was like there was no escape. And you did too – how come you waited so long to put your lights on? But then I saw you were just looking for the right place to pull me over, you were looking for the safest place! Like a real protector and I never felt like that before SHIT I would've done anything I was so freakin' grateful. And I could feel the wind was blowing on my neck and I surrendered the car, the Chrysler, onto the shoulder. It was like when you pulled me over? okay? it was the first time in my whole life that I was able to obey. It was the first time in my life I was able to pull something off like being obedient. I could feel Keith wanting to ruin it. He saw the truth of my wish.

The State Trooper hands her the letter.

STATE TROOPER: You should keep this for your records.

DONNAMARIE: Did you copy down the address? In case you want to write me back or whatever?

The State Trooper shakes his head. Exits. Donnamarie turns to wake the Cowboy.

DONNAMARIE: Hey!

The Cowboy opens his eyes and stares at her for a moment. Donnamarie stares at the letter in her good hand. She makes her way to a place away from the Cowboy and calls out to the heavens in a kind of hurry.

DONNAMARIE: KEITH! KEEEEEEEITH! KEITH! Come on! Come back! AH, KEITH! Huuh Keith. Hhhhhoooooh. Keith. Keith! I didn't do anything.

SCENE 4.

Lacey is getting ready to leave for work. She opens the refrigerator in her kitchen.

LACEY: I don't know why everything in this fridge is mixed around like that all the time now. Every DAY. God DAMN it! I'M NOT DOING it. Fuck! I KNOW I didn't do THAT.

She rearranges some things but gets frustrated. Plus it's getting late. She gets ready to leave and then does leave, slamming and locking the door behind her.

SCENE 5.

The surgeons' lounge at the Dallas Fort Worth Memorial hospital. The poet MARY OLIVER is sitting going over some files at one of the tables. Whatever it is is perplexing to her. Several minutes later NANCY enters, an authoritative new character. She is a real Clytemnestra type.

NANCY: Mary? Hello. Long time no see.

MARY: That's true. Hello, Nancy. So how are you enjoying your retirement?

NANCY: I wish I could relax! I'm now taking sculpture lessons. These sculptures I'm making. I can't do anything else. For the last couple of years all I did was decorate the house, peel wallpaper, rip up the carpets. I went through the choosing tiles, asked friends to come and help me look at different paint chips. I did all of it myself. My husband became completely hysterical one night. I wanted him to help me move a set of curio cabinets out of his t.v. room because the new carpet was arriving the next day. They had been on back order and I wanted to be ready. He screamed at me like a woman and shaking all over from head to foot. He said anything bad that had happened to me in my life I had brought on myself.

MARY: Hih hih. But now you're making sculpture.

NANCY: *(finishing putting something in her mouth)* When I walked into the first sculpture class I was the last to arrive. I had arrived late. I had also missed the first couple of classes, and everyone had set up shadow boxes, models, still lives. I walked in and took my seat; everyone was already set up. I began to take out my things. Had I been doing this my entire life, even though I had never taken a sculpture class before? It was just like walking in to the operating room! I was instantly completely at home. Going in to the material, like going in to the body. Putting the chisel to the stone. There are no coffee breaks once you put that scalpel to the skin! The other students getting up, walking around and chatting. For me? Eight or nine hours at a stretch without a thought.

MARY: Hih.

NANCY: You can't close it up and leave until you've finished what you went in to do! And you never know what you will find. You just can't know. It's never what you think, no matter what the tests have shown or anything else – imaging, sonograms. What you expect: never.

MARY: Mmmm. Mm-hmm.

NANCY: So I cancelled our trip to Alaska. We were going to take a cruise with our son and granddaughter. I've hardly seen them or anyone else since I retired, I've only wanted to sculpt without any other sort of bother. True, true . . . Howard's asked me to come in and help with the review since, after all, I'm still on the Board. Apparently the nurses are grumbling and there's talk of a strike. How selfish. Damnable nuisances if you ask me. Hardly worth their weight in dogdirt the lot of them! When I look at those foolish, clumsy nurses and think that they could be capable of starting a revolution, I think about my house. I think they could sue me and take my house from me. And I become completely and blindly enraged. I could spit into their vaginas. Registered nuisances. Laying about in the empty rooms watching television while patients roll in their own filth. Wearing big rabbit costumes for Halloween. Imagine! You're coming out of anesthesia: a human sized rabbit – writing names like Penny and Carol on the dry-erase board and switching morphine cartridges like there's nothing the matter. The lot of them. I had some, you'll never believe it. In surgery. Now I wasn't in hand surgery, I was in throat surgery. Pretty hard to get your clamp mixed up with your hemostat. But I tell you, these slags couldn't tell their own tits from the tumors thrown at the wall.

I started my shifts five, sometimes four in the morning, and afterward I'd have to go around to all the families. Ha! One time, when I was doing onco, this fellow had the nerve to ask me if I thought he'd be able to go out on his dock by summer. What do you say to that. Maybe if that's where they're going to sprinkle your ashes, Bert. It got to be too much for me in the end. Walking into a room where people have been waiting for hours to ask you all sorts of desperate, stupid questions. Don't know any of the terminology, you've got to explain everything to them as if they were some kind of little babies in a kindergarten and they get mad at ME when they misunderstand. Think I'm lying yet! Wives hanging on to my arm, men trying to bully me into giving them details they don't want to hear or can't comprehend. I began to see that there are two different breeds of humans, Mary. Us, and them. And I couldn't stand to be in the same room with them anymore. I left.

Pause

MARY: Nancy.

NANCY: Yes, Mary.

MARY: What made you want to become a surgeon. In the first place. When did you know that that's what you wanted to do.

NANCY: When I was about eight years old my sister and I went out into the yard to do our chores one afternoon after school and found the chickens all lying around on the ground dying. Chickens are not intelligent animals, Mary. They're one step above reptiles ever look at their legs? (*aside, significantly*) They're just. Absolutely. Squamous. (*once again to Mary*) . . . Anyhow, they had taken it upon themselves that day for some reason to start eating the grass of all things, and it was stuck in their throats choking them. Idiots. There must have been twenty three or so of them. Half a year's Sunday dinners laying out to waste in the yard on one afternoon because of their own stupidity. So we sliced their throats open – nice, quick, elegant cuts for a six and an eight-year-old – pulled the grass out and sewed them back up, and the damned things lived, those stupid chickens, every last one of them! And that was that. Everything I did after that was pointed deliberately toward the sole purpose of becoming a throat surgeon until the day I became one.

MARY: And your sister?

NANCY: She ended up committing suicide by setting herself on fire out by the garbage heap. Only my father was home at the time.

Pause

MARY: I'd love to see your paintings.

NANCY: SCULPTURES.

MARY: Uhh! Sculptures. Sorry!

NANCY: And the geranium pots. I'll show you. You'll have to come by the house sometime. My husband won't like that, mmt. You'll have to come when he's out.

MARY: Some other time.

NANCY: Y'ap.

Nancy pulls out some notes to go over. For a brief moment Mary is rather left hanging, and so returns to her own paperwork. At some point Lacey jumps out from under one of the tables in the lounge and surprises them.

LACEY: I heard everything you said, Dr. Hastings! EVERYTHING!

NANCY: So? So what. Who are you anyway. I don't have anything to hide . . .

LACEY: It's not like it's anything I didn't already know! And Mary, I'm surprised at you. How do you even know Dr. Nancy Hastings?

MARY: I've known Nancy for years. We're friends. Or at least we're getting to be friends. Why were you hiding under the table, Lacey? What were you hoping to hear? I know her through Howard and several of the projects here at the hospital. Are you? Are you supposed to be here?

LACEY: You know what, Mary? After you left my place that other night? After you all left that other night I really came to a point. I may have even said to Howard and Sonja that there were going to be some changes in my whole thing. And you know something? I'm glad you're here with Hastings, because it confirms something for me that I was trying not to think about you because I didn't think I was being fair.

MARY: *(a little bored and not a little irritated)* And what would that be?

LACEY: You know, when I first met you I had a strange little feeling. For one thing there was never any telling what you were ever actually thinking. And everyone seemed to like and – respect you, so I just went along with it and figured I'd catch on to why you were so likeable and respectable in good time.

NANCY: Well, I think I'd rather . . . go . . . than –

LACEY: *(moving to block her)* Oh, no you don't! You sit right back down! This is just as much for you! You're the same kind of woman, just like that. Credit for credit. You and your 'p'aintings. Or whatever.

The 'p' in paintings is accompanied with great emphasis and a little spittle which lands in the corner of Nancy's eye and confirms something for her about Lacey, and about the situation.

Nancy calmly and contemptuously wipes the spittle away, as

NANCY: Sculpture. I make . . . sculpture.

LACEY: Oh! OH! Well, 'p'ardon me!

This time there is a little more spittle. Nancy laughs silently, glances briefly up to the ceiling and then blots the new landing of spittle with a kleenex which happened to be tucked into her sleeve. She then levels her condescending gaze back at Lacey. As far as Nancy is concerned, Lacey has made her point for her and so she can just listen, or pretend to listen, or even pretend to pretend to listen, in a self-satisfied way until Lacey has spent her ridiculous and incoherently-founded antagonism.

LACEY: I bet they're just 'p'erfect aren't they! Your stupid 'p'aintings!

NANCY: *(measured, levelingly, witheringly, as Lacey continues her spittle-enhanced epithets)* You listen to me you little . . . nurse. // Sculptures. I have retained my elected seat on the Board of Directors and Advisors of this hospital, and when I say jump they say how-hi Dr. Hastings how-hi. I have a country house, central air and vacuum hook-ups throughout all, I am platinum level on everything, and I never sleep on the same sheets more than two nights in a row. And let me let you know EF WHY I – RIGHT HERE that my vote counts – BEYOND. So you just watch it. Don't get PUSHY. Missy.

LACEY: *(cont'd)* 'P'athetic. 'C'om 'p'letely 'p'athetic. . . Oh, how im 'p'ressive. . . A 'p'ot to 'p'iss in. . . 'P'ee 'p'ee 'p'oo-'p'ie! 'P'ee 'p'ee 'p'oo-'p'ie! 'P'lease. Oh, 'p'lease. 'P'uh-lease! 'P'uh-LEASE!

A pause as they catch their breath and assess what is happening, what has happened.

The future is unclear.

HOWARD enters.

HOWARD: *(shyly)* Lacey. Hello. What are you doing – Mary. Dr. Hastings. Hello, good to see you. Is – Lacey?

LACEY: Oh, Howard – Oh, my God Howard it's happening again. I'm being so mean to them and I can't –

She wavers between reaching for him, and covering her face in horror and confusion.

He wavers between going to her, explaining something somehow to the other two women, and leaving the room altogether. He carries a legal sized manila file folder in his hand.

HOWARD: You know I'm going on sabbatical.

NANCY: Sabbatical?! How are you going to manage that. What about the review!

MARY: And what about contract negotiations? We're going to really need you there, Howard.

Lacey sinks to the floor, in the meantime. She tries to crawl, slowly, back under the table she popped out from under earlier.

HOWARD: I know. Lacey –

LACEY: *(whimpering)* I wanted to make a new thing. I thought – I was wanting to see the whole, thing as a new opportunity.

HOWARD: I know. I know, Lacey.

MARY: I'm going to go. // We can talk about this later.

LACEY: *(cont'd) (from under the table now)* For something better. I'll be at the contract negotiations, Mary.

HOWARD: *(to himself, to Lacey, to Mary and as an aside)* Yes.

NANCY: Howard! What the hell is going on here? Has this place flipped its LID? // Are you going right down the TOILET?

LACEY: I'll be there with bells on.

MARY: Nancy, it's really best if we just go.

NANCY: No. No I want some answers. This man is supposed to be running this hospital.

Mary exits, shrugging and unseen by the others.

NANCY: *(cont'd)* This is a HOSPITAL. A HOSPITAL, HOWARD. Now, if this woman needs some help, let us get it for her. Lets. At the very least. Write her a referral. But what you are – WHAT THE HELL ARE YOU doing?

Howard has turned away from her and has put both hands up on the wall over the table.

He is trying to do some kind of quiet personal breathing exercise, trying to send some kind of energy to Lacey underneath the table. The usually too-rapid-to-see blinking of the fluorescent lights of the lounge becomes apparent.

NANCY: Jesus Christ. God damn it.

Nancy takes Howard's manila folder away from him, looks at it, looks at him, storms out of the lounge. She tries to slam the door, but it is the kind of door with an air cylinder so her initial yank ends impotently and the door remains agape, closing on its own time, much more softly than Nancy intended, and long after she is long gone.

ACT Y

SCENE 1.

Sonja sits together with Milcha's assistants GARRY and Figgie in an undesignated place. Garry, as it turns out, is a bit flip when he is not working for Milcha.

SONJA: Howard's left me.

GARRY: What?

SONJA: It's fairly certain.

GARRY: Oh, how do you know?

SONJA: I'm almost completely positive.

GARRY: But I asked you how!

SONJA: *(cont'd)* I can't fight it. Who am I to want to fight it?

GARRY: Well you're a // PERSON for one thing –

SONJA: What's taken place now is irrevocable. I can't make anything happen or not happen and that's something that other people never realize until it's time to be devastated. Everything has to be devastated and obliterated.

GARRY: Shuh!

SONJA: I don't understand the resistance people have, it's the most stupid waste of energy. During the last year of our relationship I've kept a fantasy waiting for a nearly full-grown daughter of Howard's to show up. A daughter he's never known.

Maybe he sensed I was having these thoughts and that's why he's left?

GARRY: No. Clearly he's going through immense, uncharted changes. And he feels // that he needs to do it on his own.

SONJA: – for some reason –

FIGGIE: I didn't tell Milcha about this by the way.

SONJA: Uh? // No, of course not.

FIGGIE: No. She thinks I'm at a shower.

SONJA: Uf. I'm almost completely against baby showers.

GARRY: *(nodding enthusiastically)* Oh for sure, as am I, and bridal showers. There's hardly any way for them not to be completely evil events.

SONJA: Yuh. I would tend to agree so much.

FIGGIE: So what should we do.

SONJA: Well, I'm not exactly sure. I was waiting to talk to Howard about it, but, as I was saying, it really seems like he's left me. A glass was there on the coffee table when I got there, and I've always loved a sweating glass on a glass top // table.

GARRY: Oh, that's so TRUE right of course! Me too!

SONJA: No coasters, no napkins linting all apart or bunching up underneath. At first I thought he was somewhere in another room. I didn't feel like going to find him, I think I wanted him to walk back in and discover me sitting by his drink. I hung on to that idea for a long, long time. I rearranged myself: how did I want to be found?

GARRY: Oh I've done that! // You know that can be great actually!

SONJA: And maybe I focused too much on the ice cubes. I just saw them dissolve – in their gradual way they dissolved, became part of the drink, and, in a sense, ended it?

GARRY: *(remembering to take some vitamin C and then taking it)* Sure –

SONJA: I didn't think it was possible for him to let them melt like that, to just leave utterly before the ice cubes even melted. I thought he would come back sometime while the drink was still cold, finish it. Explain to me what was going on, THEN leave, if that was what was happening.

GARRY: IF.

SONJA: I never checked the other rooms, I just stayed there with the drink. That's the short version. Basically, I'm saying I don't know what to do, and I haven't made a plan of who to go to after this happens.

FIGGIE: So what should we do. Now, it looks to me like there are a lot of people that we need to make see things the way we're seeing them.

SONJA: And I'm just sitting here talking about staring at melting ice cubes.

FIGGIE: I mean, I just –

SONJA: And that's not the most effective way of going about that kind of process . . . ?

FIGGIE: No no! Well, maybe not. Not on the face of it. But okay who's to say that can't be part of it? Who's to say that if we're talking about a process? That that process can't include all sorts of different perspectives! You know maybe it's just about reassembling priorities . . .

SONJA: Hmm. Hmph.

Pause

FIGGIE: I mean the issue with Milcha. A washed-up has-been when you're still packing the supper clubs and piling on encores like layers of wedding cake? All those screaming fans? But she's insisting.

SONJA: Well, then we've got to try it. Something. With or without Howard. There's a point where your personal violence and struggles have to stop figuring in to the point you're trying to make or the actions you're trying to take.

FIGGIE: Sonja? I couldn't agree with you more.

They embrace, then stand clasping hands to elbows. A long pause.

GARRY waits, wide-eyed, then gravely applies the very smallest amount of lip balm.

FIGGIE suddenly turns away from them, addresses the entire audience. SONJA doesn't seem to notice. She begins doing some other preparatory activity altogether.

SCENE 1a.

FIGGIE: I never got to a point in my life where I could sit with the adults at the cookout and relax by talking with other adults. I really actually can't stand it. Too many . . . conversational pitfalls. Too many painful stabs with the 'friendly' talk. It just MATTERS too much what you say or don't say. Watch the jokes, but don't try going without jokes either. People say, "oh, c'mon by and have a beer," as if it's going to be so nice and relaxing – you're just going to stroll right over and really enjoy yourself – but what they don't tell you is you'll have to interact with them. I don't want to talk, okay? What is there to talk about with you? I-want-to-jump-in-your-pool. Right off. No beating around the bush, I'm already WEARING in my bathing suit, okay dollface? I'll do my own exploring in the house thanks – NOT the "tour," "the tour," – I'm fine to grab the food I want, you know curl up and take a nap, go home. That's what I want, and that's how I want it. Otherwise, you're wasting my time. Don't waste my time. How can it have become about sitting and talking? The way I see it: If you're talking? Someone's getting feelings hurt.

Figgie turns to face the Cowboy, who has now appeared inexplicably, and is handed a cold can of beer by him. They drink, eyeing one another suspiciously.

Then there is a

SCENE 2.

for Mary and her hand-held tape recorder

MARY: Susurrous. A slow sad susurrous rustle like the wind fingering the pines. A murmurous brook. A soughing wind in the pines. System of systems! Binding arbitration. Lock out/walk out.

Pause

MARY: *(cont'd)* Nirdvandva: freedom from opposites.

Pause

MARY: *(cont'd)* Recumbent: utterly reliant on the absence of hostility in a given environment . . . Feminine . . . ?

Pause

MARY: *(cont'd)* Procumbent: crawling face down along the ground as roots or pipes . . . Elderly . . . ?

Pause

MARY: *(cont'd)* Incumbent.

Pause

MARY: *(cont'd)* Cucumber.

SCENE 3.

Milcha enters her rehearsal studio, unwraps herself of excessive garments. It appears she has just come in from the cold, only it's not cold outside. An answering machine message from MORTIE is heard playing. Unwrapped, she wilts into a wheelchair.

MORTIE: All I'm saying, Kiddo, is that I know these networks, and they're going to say, "Who do you got for the kids?" I'm saying if you think the red tape we've run into with the commissioners is bad, we're talking advertising spots that have to be filled, and if you want prime time, I know we had talked about showtime or disney, and I don't know if you've talked to anyone about a budget. But the budget determines who you can get. In the old days you heard a lot of "I'll do it for free." And you just don't hear that anymore. I mean these people are getting PAID to eat in certain restaurants for the love of God! And handsomely!

Milcha is already talking to him on the phone as the message continues to play.

MILCHA: And I'm telling YOU, Mor-tie, I've already squared that away with Clive Bristol. He's going to open up his entire stable of popular young recording artists for our use. Gary L. Pughblen of the World Communication Awards has agreed to produce the special. And he's doing the budget as we speak. Enough already. We've talked in circles. I mean I just can't. And that's not my JOB, Mor-tie. No such luck. I've given FIGGIE the rest of the day off. Oh, there's a shower somewhere. *(an annoyed gesture, increasingly exhausted)* Uch! Oh I know all about you and bridal showers – the perfume, the designs, the schemes of all the women. Ya-huh. The shrieking. That's right. You've got to get up pretty early in the morning, Mor-tie. I've known you too long. My voice. I've GOT to rest. I've got to REST. Mortie.

She hangs up on him, looks around. She gazes at the piano. She gives the wheelchair wheels one defeated push toward it and finishes the rest of the way wanly pulling it along with tiny footsteps like a beleaguered Flintstonian. She resignedly stands, plays a few notes, wilts once again into the wheelchair. Then suddenly she is banging the keys of the piano with her fist.

MILCHA: Damn it! Damn it! Damn it! Damn it!

She pauses briefly and then wheelingly punches the air, her own legs and her head several times, very hard, but in an exploratory way. She sits quietly panting for a moment and considers what she has just done. A few moments go by. She presses gingerly on the places that have suffered impact from the sudden fists: her head, her legs, the piano keys.

MILCHA: *(singing either a cappella, or with her own terrible piano accompaniment, in a strange hollow operatic voice we have not heard from her and which reveals to us something toward knowing her real age)* Oh, Shenandoah I long to hear you Away, you rolling river Oh, Shenandoah, I long to hear you Away, oh, away across the wide Missouri

The answering machine beeps again. We hear the unmistakably distinctive voice of the Large Cowboy Statue.

VOICE of LARGE COWBOY STATUE: Sonja! Sonja how are you. WHERE ARE YOU! How come I haven't heard from you – you gave me one message when you got back, I haven't heard from you LISTEN. I'm walkin' around on the streets here with Jean and Bistek ME, JEAN and BISTEK! We want – YOU! We WANT you! Where are you! The three of us. Wanna get with you. Ok? That's all I want to say, call me. Ha ha! Bye, darlin'.

MILCHA: *(futilely calling out to the answering machine)* You have the wrong number. She was only staying here for a limited time.

SCENE 4.

Nancy puts the finishing touches on two cowboy sculptures in the sculpture studio classroom, while Sean and his man family have a hushed discussion with a LAWYER.

SCENE 5.

Lacey's apartment, empty.

After quite a pause, a key in the door.

Howard enters, closes and locks the door behind him. He looks vaguely around, closes his eyes, takes a few breaths, bursts into tears. He takes himself over to the refrigerator and solemnly unzips his pants. He begins taking different items out of the refrigerator and, still weeping, rubbing them against his genitals in a torn and agonized way, and placing them back into the refrigerator. He repeats for a few minutes and the rubbing with the items gathers vigor. He is still crying, though now with joy. He closes the refrigerator door and leans against it with the foremost part of his body. He closes his eyes, recovers his composure to a certain degree, and then exits, locking the door carefully behind him.

ACT Z

SCENE 1.

The executive administrative conference room at the Fort Worth Radisson Hotel. Set details are vague. There are, however, water glasses and yellow legal pads.

After considerable delay MARY OLIVER takes the center podium. She reads from a script.

The things she says are not her own words, though – strangely – she tries to try half-heartedly to play it off as if they are her own words.

MARY: "Now is the time for the Nurse's Contract to be negotiated. Let's see what's on the table here. Oh, okay. First, the pensions. The pensions are on the table."

NURSES UNION answers in an incantation, with Lacey screaming the loudest, far above the volume of the others. She looks disheveled and misused.

NURSES UNION with LACEY: Take the pensions off the table!

MARY: "No." "No way." That's not the way to start these, screaming like that?

NURSES UNION with LACEY: Take the pensions off the table! That's like taking away our paychecks.

MARY: Okay, I will say this, okay: "If you go on strike," as I understand it, "you will be taking away your own paychecks." So, "do not go on strike. We're talking about what's INDUSTRY STANDARD. It's like a 401K." Uh, it looks like that's all the time we have for the negotiations. In closing, "I have two words for you. Binding arbitration."

Uh-huh. Okay? Uh, I'll leave you with that. Now next up, "we will open the floor to discussion and appeals." That is, anything besides the contract negotiations with the Nurses Union.

The floor is now opened to discussion and appeals. Nurses Union disperses, muttering.

Lacey is trying to get them to band together and take a stronger stand, but for some reason has lost her ability to speak. She can only gesture. And because of her disheveled, worsened appearance and overly-desperate manner, no one pays any real attention to her. Everyone avoids her. In the meantime,

NANCY: *(to Mary)* That was a MESS, Mary!

MARY: I'm going by the book okay Nancy.

Figgie and Sonja are brought in by the GUARDS. They are shackled and swaddled and are thrown to the feet of all the masters.

NANCY: NOW what.

MARY: What is this? What is the problem? Sonja?

SONJA: We need the help of a great surgeon. Her name is Dr. Nancy Hastings.

MARY: But this isn't the right context for those kinds of requests.

SONJA: *(to Nancy, ignoring Mary)* We tried to come to your house, but the security system was too tight.

NANCY: *(nearly to herself, with a profound, somewhat unnatural satisfaction)* It's a system of systems.

She stands, with gravity and formality, almost as if she is embodying an entire graduating class. She regards not Figgie or Sonja but the entire assemblage.

NANCY: (*cont'd*) Assembled! I shall address you. You shall bear my adjudication.

FIGGIE: (*speaking on behalf of Milcha*) I speak on behalf of this woman, Milcha. And she needs a procedure on her pneuma. She is proud, and mistrustful of doctors, and refuses a shamanistic approach even more adamantly. We must needs do it without her permission. Please!

Nancy takes a different stance as she consults her inner position. When she has finished,

NANCY: I know this woman, this Milcha, have heard her sing, in a memory from long, long ago, early on in the now endless years of my marriage. We sat at a table with many others and ignored the supper before us. And again later, the televised broadcasts in the den. We remembered that we were Americans and so innately longed for the open road. I agree to at least sculpt her likeness in clay, possibly even marble.

A little uncertain of what the actual upshot is, but not wanting to push their luck, Figgie and Sonja bow their heads in a tentative, perplexed gratitude. A gesture of Nancy's assures them that their audience with her is definitively over. Sonja steals a glance to Howard. He looks away, then bows his own head. After a moment, Nancy resumes her seat.

Figgie and Sonja awkwardly regain their feet, unhelped. Since the guards do not seem to know enough to remove the appellants, Howard takes the reluctant initiative and gently guides them out by their elbows. Sonja does not seem to know whether to relish his touch.

Donnamarie appears, in a strange white wedding gown, with the Cowboy, who wears an orange prison jumpsuit. Her head is now permanently pitched forward so that her chin rests on her clavicle. She holds her good arm tight to her ribs like a chicken leg, and speaks and walks with difficulty. Sean Crosby and his Man Family trail behind them.

DONNAMARIE: I was mistreated at this hospital! *(tries pointing at Sean)* And so was he! We are ready for justice! You know? A little FUCKING justice around here, right Sean?

SEAN: Yeah . . . But I mean, I thought –

He looks to his man family. All are at a loss.

DONNAMARIE: (*cont'd*) I've got all your bills telling me what I owe. I didn't want you to think I hadn't got them. But we're not going to be paying up until we get some justice. This is like a hold up. But instead it's a hold up for justice and some fucking respect and some fairness.

She grabs the Cowboy's hand with her unswollen one.

DONNAMARIE: This is my husband now, okay? I'm not all lone anymore! When I go, he'll be by my side!

COWBOY: We didn't always. We weren't sure. But now we know. But, you see, now it just can't be. Except inside us.

He hangs his head in sorrow and gratitude.

NANCY: (*sorely reproachful*) Disastrous, Mary.

No one else knows what to say. Pause. Mary shrugs and dutifully re-assumes the podium. Howard re-enters the room, wiping his hands on a piece of waste.

MARY: Um, well we have one member of the Board of Directors who is leaving us. Howard, will you step up? We hope you won't forget where you came from!

HOWARD: Th-thank you and I just want to say thank you to everyone who I've worked with over these most satisfying years. It's been very satisfying. For so many years, all of us. Working side by side together, receiving, communicating. Making a difference. I can't thank you enough. It's impossible to measure what it means to me. And to those that come here in the future, may they experience the same with their own colleagues. Bless, bless all of you, alright? And don't forget all the work we did to get here! We made it happen together! Motivation, responsibility, premeditation. Impulse. Who can say unless you're there in the moment. Why we do things. In a moment of passion, in cold blood. We know not what we do when we're doing it, we're just acting on a feeling, on a knowledge of what we have before us to do. If we're in tune. It's not about what's right or wrong, because what might "seem" "wrong" can be the right thing that NEEDS to HAPPEN, and it's really up to you in the end. No one can do what you do.

MARY: And now it's time to find out how Dallas Fort Worth Memorial did on the Review. I know we're all curious. Welcome, Review Panel.

REVIEW PANEL files in, takes its seats. Each member of Review Panel is, strangely, in mask. Ancient Greek mask. The PowerPoint projector is fired up. Review Panel speaks, as a chorus.

REVIEW PANEL: We are the review panel. As you know, your hospital has been under review.

We have tested your compliance to certain codes. Are you wondering how you did? Or do you feel like you have a pretty good idea? HA ha HA ha HA ha ah HA! HAQU! HAQU HAYug HIN HINREN HINDREN DILJuN We came, we showed up and we tested you. We observed your methods and your compliances. We took note of your adherence to procedural guidelines.

We measured the discrepancies, we took note of the times and places where you fell short of concurrent sanctioned ideals. HANQ XX HANQ XX ssheeumsh.

Review Panel gathers its papers in canon, in neat, conclusive piles all along the surface of the long conference table. Review Panel reads, again as a chorus, from the first page.

REVIEW PANEL: (*cont'd*) We have concluded that you didn't eat what you needed to eat. You ate what everyone else was eating and you were weak in your choices. You ate that which made you bloated and cranky, if not right away, then inexorably the entire next day. You followed the nearest example, got lazy, let go, ate what smelled good the moment before you agreed to eat it. You didn't eat what you needed to eat. (*now speaking directly to the audience*) And the worst failure is that you knew better. You knew better. You had even agreed with the theories. You went so far as to not have had qualm with the theories. You could have done so much better. And so: there will be penalties, because now we are going to start setting off the marching orders all around to you. Wait and see who gets a pink slip over the coming days. And wait and see who gets reamed a new asshole by the commission.

Prepare.

Review Panel has spoken. It rises, bangs gavels, and salutes, all in canon, and files out. Everyone looks around at each other, mystified and insecure.

The whole thing becomes a huge media event. Donnamarie and Sean are talking to the press. The media crowd and crowd in.

At last the crowd of media opens up so that the oracle may enter the souls of the audience. Their souls are ripped open mercilessly and the oracle enters them a little roughly. In most cases, the audience cries out in pain at the brutality of the incursion, then whimpers ever so softly, in helpless submission to this inexplicable and disordered force, this force so much greater and more nimble than themselves. In others the audience merely looks upon this same force with disdain and a bored recognition and then proceeds to chat disengagedly amongst itself. In one instance, the audience stands up and fights. But is later crushed completely. And in two other instances audiences, similarly, are massacred. One particular audience grapples with it on the surface out of an intense inner conflict that bespeaks an inability to differentiate between meaning and opinion, which somehow dwarfs the actual taking of its soul. In another, not a sound is made. The audience becomes more inexplicable than the force itself, but is at the same time very, very ordered and very, very masculine. In a certain instance the audience greets the despoil of its soul with a similar disdain as did one of the other audiences mentioned earlier, but this disdain is disguised by great respect, deference, and an insistent iron imperative of effeminate politeness. A certain rather remarkable audience accepts the taking with calm, dignity and good humor, and a profound and unfounded sense of understanding.

ACT Q

SCENE 1.

Whichever audience this is, they are exhausted. But they have also had a nice dinner. But their throats are raw & sore after shoving and shoving the food down in great haste in order to pay and get back to the theater to make this new act.

When the curtain rises it reveals a low valley covered with dense woods. In the middle of the wood is a lake, with a refreshing breeze caressing the trees. Mary is there, wearing her usual clothing, which now looks more en place. She holds her tape recorder in her hand but does not speak into it.

MARY: This kingdom of trees imprisons me. Nature is no longer enough. Look at these boughs! Hardly mature and already breaking off, breaking down. My preparations are useless and everyone knows it. All that time spent at the Burgtown Institute, delivering humorous lectures and after-dinner speeches. I'm appalled when I remember how I entertained them. There's a war happening up here in these treetops and the leftover corpses cling to the bark. They don't know what else to do. They are the ones who couldn't transform. The ones as could are wiggling and wriggling in their safe little buntings of brown membrane filled to bursting, twitching this way and that. They don't know what the heck is going on. What's worse. What's the worse that my glands respond to them? And you'll call that a glandular response. And all the mystery of our bodies and minds lies in the glands – women, and men. Children. Animals. Our glands which live and secrete and fight it out amongst themselves over something unknown.

A smoked limousine pulls up. The back door opens and Milcha steps out, looking confused and disabused. An aluminum walker with tennis balls on the two back legs and wheels on the front is tossed from an unseen hand on to the gravel behind her. As Milcha scrambles to retrieve it, two more cars pull up in a grating scratch of gravel and dust. Sean and his Man Family step out of one of them, and the Cowboy, the two Cowboy Statues and the State Trooper step out of the other one.

Milcha looks at them nervously.

MILCHA: Where is Figgie?

MARY: Figgie couldn't come.

MILCHA: *(suddenly, ignoring or not hearing Mary)* SONJA! I want SONJA!

MARY: No. Sonja is busy.

MILCHA: No!

SMALL COWBOY STATUE: Quiet.

MILCHA: Well, I won't be quiet!

Pause

MILCHA: Not while I'm so upset! That driver better go pick up my attorney! Mor-tie Felcher! Suite 1558 Cottonwoodblossom Complex. I hope he knows!

She looks for a seat. No one moves. There are no seats. She spots Mary.

MILCHA: Oh, I know you! Well, you certainly look more en place in this kind of setting. Those clothes of yours. For me? It's wretched this locale. And by the way, what did you know about this!

MARY: I learned about it at the hospital where Sonja's boyfriend works. But they're keeping it under the table.

MILCHA: Oh, that is shit. I don't feel like this now. Take me home. One of you. One of you big damned fools.

A certain physical struggle ensues between Milcha and the group of men.

MILCHA: I'm not going through with it!

She loses the struggle quickly. A pause.

MARY: You do know that hitherto something has always prevented you from going here.

MILCHA: Damn you people.

MARY: But this time you are already half way through your plan.

MILCHA: Plan! This ain't MY 'plan,' honey. I've got no idea what're you talking about! You are WASTING MY LIFE. If there is one thing I cannot stand it's having my life wasted. I know about out-of-sorts, at-a-loss, sixes-and-sevens, box-and-cox! I can't help myself when your kind of people waste my life with your stupid human obligations that you like SO much to impose. I can not stand another bullshit minute of it. And I know I'm dead and I know all about it. You fucking fuckers. I wanted to die. You made me want to die. You shits. I hate you all.

Milcha, finished, reluctantly approaches the lake. Mary and the men follow with measured steps. The atmosphere grows uncanny.

Suddenly a light gust of wind passes over the surface of the water, which ripples darkly. She cries out in terror.

MILCHA: That light gust of wind, passing over the surface of the water, which ripples darkly. It's an unseen presence. I know what it is. I can't deal with it! I don't have the energy. I know it's there. I can't stand to have to deal with this kind of shit right now. Oh, God. Oh, God just leave me here. Don't leave me here. Please. I want to be alone. GET OUT! Sonja, don't leave me alone. I have so much hatred. Please come back.

She screams.

SCENE 2.

Howard and Lacey. Howard stands with an open fly in front of Lacey's open refrigerator, apparently in the process of explaining himself.

HOWARD: Still, I do care who knows. I'd rather they didn't know.

LACEY: Well what am I supposed to do now that I know?

Pause.

LACEY: And, you know, what about how I feel?

HOWARD: Lacey, I don't know if you will be willing to see it this way, but for me it is about meaning. What I'm doing here, in your apartment, when I come in here and you aren't home. I'm compelled to do it. I know it's wrong by our common everyday standards. Sometimes it terrifies me and even rips my soul from limb to limb. But – and I really do believe this, Lacey – I think I'm answering to something beyond all that. Maybe it sounds dumb. Or square. Lacey, nevermind all that – I think, I have reason to believe, that what I'm doing here, here in your apartment refrigerator, when I come in here unbeknownst to you and rub these items onto my bare genitals, is that I'm making art.

LACEY: Whuchh?? Fuck. Howard! – how can this be art! How can it! It's not even a painting or anything!

HOWARD: Okay. Please calm down.

LACEY: This is like incredibly arrogant, Howard. Who the hell do you think you are?

HOWARD: But I learned this information from a foreign voice that was inside my head. She spoke to me, very quietly. A woman's voice. Lacey, it wasn't you, or Sonja, or my mother, or anyone. Nancy Hastings, no – it wasn't her either. It could have been, but it wasn't. I had never heard this voice before in regular life. She came from the outside and from inside. But I had perhaps heard her before, I had just never been in a quiet enough place to listen.

LACEY: Jesus God I mean if you want to make art this bad why don't you go with Nancy Hastings I mean you could do your own thing in that class, you know whatever. You could even use cadavers or something, I've heard of people doing stuff like that.

HOWARD: Lacey, I can be free this way, and I can make history.

LACEY: But this is private. It's my private property.

Pause

HOWARD: *(still on the former topic of himself and his 'art')* What do you think it is Lacey. If it's not art. What do YOU think it is. Let me ask that.

LACEY: It's pathological!

HOWARD: LACEY!

LACEY: The problem is that you think what you're doing is special, or belongs only to you, or's only from you, when really it either belongs to everyone already and is so boring and brutal once you're really looking at it with any kind of realistic perspective or it doesn't even apply because it never makes it outside from my kitchen refrigerator. Even if you found a way for it to make you successful. It's not art, Howard.

HOWARD: WELL THEN WHAT IS IT THEN LACEY?

LACEY: It's

Pause

LACEY: It's

Longer pause

HOWARD: (*thinking he has defeated her*) Ok then.

LACEY: It's swinishness.

This is a real slap in the face to Howard.

LACEY: To tell you the truth Howard I think you better get out of here because I am feeling really on edge. You are really pushing me and you just can't imagine how much you shouldn't be saying all this right now. And I'm already having all these problems. And I don't know where they're going to end me up! And I know that I'm speaking pretty sensibly about it now – but later on this is going to cause me a real kind of breakdown. I know it! It's all related and connected and no one sees it and no one admits it. They CAN'T see it. Oh, my stomach is tightening up into a knot! It's going to make me do something, Howard. Because it's too much pressure. I'm going to start screaming again, screaming at people. Hurting them. Hurting their feelings. Or worse. Their bodies. Not worse for them, worse for me! I hurt them because I can't hurt myself properly! God dammit Howard this is really going to fuck me up!

The doorbell rings. It's FIGGIE.

FIGGIE: Sonja is at war with Milcha. I thought you should know. Milcha is fighting from beyond – the grave? I'm not sure. I can't bring myself to believe that I didn't know she died – plus as it turns out she's some kind of deity. I think I always sensed that. I've worked for her for a long time. I don't know whether Sonja stands a chance or not. I don't know her all that well. But then someone else said that Dr. Hastings is behind the whole thing, and that she's brainwashed Sonja. You'd better come with me, uh, both of you.

Exeunt.

SCENE 3.

The gates of Nancy's fortress. The renowned geranium pots.

Nancy's long-suffering husband, CHARLES, beside several bags of rotting and half-eaten groceries.

CHARLES: When I think of all the fundraising events that have happened here. The most heightened attraction of standing on any donor page worth its vellum. 'GLIMMERING GOLDEN HEADLINERS' CIRCLE (contribution of $500,000 or more): All of the above, plus An invitation to a special event in a private home.' So many times that meant our house. It wasn't hard to detect the subtle differences of affiliation, persuasion. Vivid prospects of status and influence wafting in with the catering trucks in the late morning sun. Preeminence itself released in heady pulses into the tents in the early evening, the most celebrated of prominence at the forefront. Lavish speeches, placid but plentiful applause. These were the ancient rituals of a long, long time ago. They seem so naïve and primitive looking back on them now. The walls of my secret garden place are crumbling now.

Mary enters, holding an ice pack to the top of her head.

MARY: You must be Nancy's husband.

CHARLES: I have a name. Charles. My name is Charles Isherwood Hastings II. I'm not just Nancy's husband and that's all I'm good for, you know. I'm my own man. A self-made man.

MARY: Alright Charles. You'll have to forgive me. I'm not feeling well. I'm under psychic attack.

CHARLES: Well, you'll have to pull yourself out of it or pretend like it's not happening if you plan on presenting yourself to Nancy. She abhors that kinda thing.

MARY: Is she in there?

CHARLES: Oh she's in there all right. She sent me out for provisions a few days ago and when I came back there were guards posted at the entrance who refused to admit me. It's not the first time something like this has happened, but she's never gone this far before.

MARY: I wonder if they'll let me in. Who else is in there, do you know?

CHARLES: Day before yesterday I saw a group of – people? – go in and they were cloaked figures, and they were in mask. Some kind of preternatural review panel from what I could gather.

MARY: Yeah that'll be the Review Panel. Who else?

CHARLES: A bunch of people. Damned if I know. This is a real destination. Nancy doesn't fuck around. She's even got some hostages in there.

MARY: Oh! That'd be Sonja!

CHARLES: Y'ap. That sounds about right.

MARY: Well, that is good to know. *(sighs matter-of-factly)* So these are the legendary geranium planters.

CHARLES: These are those. Them. They weigh about a thousand pounds each. Good luck trying to lift 'em.

MARY: I thought there would be so many more of them.

CHARLES: There are, but I keep em in my secret garden place now. Away from everything else.

MARY: Look at that marvelous blue – the shape isn't the point.

CHARLES: Look at the marvelous shapes – the color doesn't even figure in.

MARY: Is this blue the same as that blue over there? Do you see any difference?

CHARLES: You're mixing the paint and you say "It's hard to get the blue of this sky."

MARY: Look what different effects these two blues have.

CHARLES: What's this blue called? – Is it 'indigo'?

MARY: You sometimes attend the color by putting your hand up to keep the outline from view; or by not looking at the outline of the thing; sometimes by staring at the object and trying to remember where you saw that color before.

CHARLES: You pay attention to the shape, sometimes by tracing it, sometimes by screwing up your eyes so you don't see the color clearly. And in lots of other ways.

MARY: I want to say: This is the sort of thing that happens while one directs one's attention to this or that.

CHARLES: But it isn't these things by themselves that make us say someone is attending on the shape, the color, and so on.

MARY: But suppose someone said:

MARY and CHARLES: I always do the same thing when I attend to/on the shape: my eye follows the outline and I feel . . .

CHARLES: And suppose this person to give someone else the sort of definition "That is called a 'circle,'" pointing to a circular object and having all these experiences –

MARY: Cannot his hearer still interpret the definition differently, even though he sees the other's eyes following the outline, and even though he feels what the other feels?

They make love.

SCENE 4.

The cemetery.

Howard brings Lacey and Figgie through the rows, searching urgently for his special stone. They are all grasping hands. Garry is also with them.

HOWARD: This way, no this way.

He finds it, but this time it's hewn, into a very matter-of-fact headstone.

HOWARD: Oh, no! That's not it! I mean, that is it, but it's been hewn! Devil-be-damned it's been hewn!

LACEY: (*reading the headstone*) "Our Milcha. 1917-2007. She had a lover's quarrel with the world." That sounds familiar. I think I've seen that one somewhere before. I think they ripped that off from someone else.

FIGGIE screams.

HOWARD: But this isn't why I brought you! Try to forget what it says for a second! This is where I had that experience, Lacey!?

Donnamarie and the Cowboy descend upon them in a dune buggy, brandishing crude but cleaned weaponry. Donnamarie is clearly near death, her face furrowed with suffering.

LACEY: I remember this woman! Look at you now! Your face is furrowed with suffering. What kind of cruel justice is that!

DONNAMARIE: Excalibur has a sharp blade.

SCENE 5.

Inside Nancy's fortress.

Nancy fingers the leaves of some plants with one hand and the string of pearls on her neck with the other.

NANCY: Ultimately I never meant to hurt anyone. It's quite merely a pursuit of exactness, nothing more. Another flute of champagne?

SONJA: No thank you.

SCENE 6.

Charles and Mary lay loosely covered with soil in on a garden patio in Charles' secret garden place, surrounded by countless geranium planters.

CHARLES: I've always had rectangles, but they were always really sharp and clear. Now, there's a rectangle that's blurry and red. I'm trying to imagine making a drawing of one of those sharp and clear rectangles like I'm used to from this blurry one.

MARY: Of course, several such sharply defined rectangles can be drawn to correspond to the indefinite one –

CHARLES: But if the colors in the original merge without a hint of any outline won't it become a hopeless task to draw a sharp picture that goes with the blurry one? Wouldn't it be:

MARY and CHARLES: Here I might just as well draw a circle or heart as a rectangle, for all the colors merge. Anything – and nothing – is right.

They make love again, showing signs of great emotional intensity.

SCENE 7.

Later on. Mary and Charles. Loosely clothed.

MARY: When I arrived here it was to take my post at Nancy's side, and aid her in the obliteration of her detractors and in the acquisition of new suppliants. But now that purpose has been swept away with the tides of lust overarching, overreaching for you, her husband. The years of thoughtless neglect on her part have only ripened you – though you are no less forbidden to me by ties of a wretched marriage to Nancy. Now her enemy, I can only hope for her swift defeat in stern death.

CHARLES: Mary. Mary, right? No one has ever made me so happy in my body. I have abandoned its previous form as a lump of useless dough and under your knowing touch have become a mighty shaft of erect and invincible muscle. I feel like a giant engorged penis and am ready to thrust my way into the dark, red, sweet tunnel of a new life with you, Mary. I had seen you before but you never noticed me, and anyway I thought you were a lesbian. And now. Let me take you again into my arms . . . submit once again, Mary, to the ferocious demands of my iron embraces . . .

MARY: Charles, later. We must focus our full presence and attention on attaining victory against Nancy. I shall not rest until we are both smeared with her blood, spurted hotly onto our living skin by her shuddering, expired heart organ.

CHARLES: Oh, Mary. Mary. You're making me dizzy. I'm really getting carried away by your enthusiasm. But won't a speedy divorce do the trick just as well?

MARY: Secured only by the certainty of her death, can we consort freely with one another. As little as you mean to Nancy, she will be loath to relinquish you to a rival's charge. But along with that certainty we will conquer outrageously vast regions of power and influence. Everything Nancy has, everything she has achieved, will be ours for the taking once she wheezes her last foul, selfish breath at our tingling hands.

CHARLES: Mary! I really never thought about it that way!

MARY: I claim you now, on this patio, Charles Isherwood Hastings II, for my own. To hell with some measly divorce, your soul is mine. Together we shall endeavor to turn cruel wife to helpless victim and lay hands on all the luscious spoils bitter frigid Nancy now withholds from our glorious possession. Oh, I am exalted – throbbing with bloodlust. I spit on myself!

She holds her arms out in front of herself in wild ecstasy.

CHARLES: Mary, I'm all yours!

A commotion is heard at the gate.

MARY: What's that commotion at the gate?

CHARLES: I don't know. I'll go look.

MARY: No, you stay here. I'll go.

She exits. When she doesn't come back immediately, Charles figures he had better straighten himself up a little bit, tucking his shirt in, smoothing down and checking his rumpled pants, his tousled hair.

Unbeknownst to him, Nancy enters through a secret door.

NANCY: Good morning, my darling.

CHARLES: YIKES! Nancy! You scared me!

NANCY: I scared you? How could you be scared of me? Your wife of so many years? I'm devoted to you. I'm doing all of this for you, my darling.

CHARLES: Nancy, what is it exactly that you are doing anyway? I'm not exactly clear on all this.

NANCY: Oh, it's nothing for you to worry about, Charles my love. Listen, I'm sorry about the lock-out, dear. I just had some details to take care of, and I knew you had your secret garden place to come to. The geraniums look like they could use some attention. Should I send Garcia out here? Or would you rather be alone. Have you had any lunch?

CHARLES: Uh . . .

NANCY: What is it, my dear? Is anything wrong?

CHARLES: Nuh . . .

NANCY: All right, I'll leave you be. I know how you love your quiet time. One more thing. I'm expecting a very large delivery of roses this afternoon. If you hear the doorbell ring. But one of the gentlemen at the door will take care of it. I adore you, Charles. You must know that . . .

She briefly handles him by his chin, exits.

Mary enters.

MARY: I heard that whole thing. I guess she still loves you. Well, I could have killed her right then and there but it seems like you could have done it yourself if you really wanted her out of the way. Look, a bunch of people I know have showed up here, and that sort of brought me to my senses. They need my help and my input, as usual. I'm not going to kill your wife for you, Charles. At least not today. If you want to get rid of her you'll have to do it yourself. You really are a wonderful man, Charles. I had an exceptional time with you here today. I suppose I just got a little carried away.

CHARLES: Well, you'll know where to find me. If anything else comes up.

Mary exits. He flumps down on a bench, a bit deflated.

SCENE 8.

The Big Battle Scene.

Nancy's fortress is stormed by an armed mob, led by Mary, Howard, Lacey, Figgie, Donnamarie and the Cowboy, Sean Crosby and his Man Family. On Nancy's side are Sonja, the Large and Small Cowboy statues, the State Trooper, Garry, and Review Panel.

SCENE 9.

The Delivery of Roses amidst the great battle, received by the depressed Charles.

From the center of the Roses appear the Pneumae of Milcha and of KEITH, Donnamarie's deceased brother. Charles accompanies them to the highest garrett of the fortress to survey the progress of the battle. At its height, they appear to the battlers. Sonja apologizes to Milcha and says she wants to get back together with Howard. Howard says it's too late, he's moved on to other things. He asks to become Nancy's sculpture assistant and she refuses. He joins Charles, and they join with the other men, led by the Pneuma of Keith. The men are all now on one side, united, and the women on the other, divided but determined to prevail over the men.

End

of the LOST ACTS

of CRIME OR EMERGENCY

Sibyl Kempson writes and performs in her own plays in New York City and the Pocono Mountains. Other titles include Potatoes of August, Zeit af der KürbisGeistNachten (or) It's a Good Life If You Don't Weaken, The Secret Death of Puppets (or) How Do Puppets Die? (or) Puppets Die in Secret, The Wytche of Problymm Plantation, Spargel Time! and This Property is BAUHAUS! Also Kyckling and Screaming, an adaptation of Henrik Ibsen's The Wild Duck, and At the Kingdom's Gate: Prelude, a translation of Knut Hamsun's Ved Rigets Port: Forspil, in progress. She has performed for many years with New York City Players and with Elevator Repair Service and also helped to establish the playwrights' groups of Joyce Cho and Machiqq. She is a graduate of the Brooklyn College MFA program that Mac Wellman teaches.

Thanks to Kristen Kosmas, Patricia Laurence, Mac Wellman.

Thanks to Bernadette Corporation.Thanks to all the ladies of Machiqq plus Torrey Hyatt.

Thanks also to Ellie Covan, Leslie Strongwater and Kimberly Brandt, Sarah Benson, Ron Berry, and Vallejo Gantner. Thanks to Mike Iveson, Jr. and Jeff Jones.

Thanks to family.

Special thanks to Karinne Keithley.

Book design: Karinne Keithley
On cover: Phyllis Dickens (photographer unknown)

53rd State Press publishes new plays and performance texts. It was founded in 2007 by Karinne Keithley. For more information, please visit www.53rdstatepress.com

All 53rd State books are available for trade and individual purchase through Small Press Distribution: www.spdbooks.org.

53rd State Press thanks Ugly Duckling Presse for distribution support. Find UDP at www.uglyducklingpresse.org